Samsung
Galaxy S23 Ultra
Camera Guide

Beginner to Expert Guide to Master Samsung Galaxy S23 Ultra Camera with Useful Professional Photography and Editing Hacks, Tips & Tricks

CARTY BINN

Copyright © 2023 **CARTY BINN**

All Rights Reserved

This book or parts thereof may not be reproduced in any form, stored in any retrieval system, or transmitted in any form by any means—electronic, mechanical, photocopy, recording, or otherwise—without prior written permission of the publisher, except as provided by United States of America copyright law and fair use.

Disclaimer and Terms of Use

The author and publisher of this book and the accompanying materials have used their best efforts in preparing this book. The author and publisher make no representation or warranties with respect to the accuracy, applicability, fitness, or completeness of the contents of this book. The information contained in this book is strictly for informational purposes. Therefore, if you wish to apply the ideas contained in this book, you are taking full responsibility for your actions.

Printed in the United States of America

TABLE OF CONTENTS

TABLE OF CONTENTS III
INTRODUCTION 1
   SO, WHAT DOES EACH CAMERA DO? 2
   GALAXY S23 ULTRA'S FOUR REAR CAMERAS INCLUDE A 200-MEGAPIXEL MAIN CAMERA 3
CHAPTER 1 5
MASTERING THE S23 CAMERA APP 5
   WHAT ARE THE 4 WAYS TO LAUNCH THE GALAXY S23 CAMERA APP? 5
   NEW FEATURES OF THE S23 SERIES CAMERA APP 6
      Main features of the camera app 6
      Night portrait and Night selfie 6
      Night video and Night selfie video 7
      Additional features 8
      Different ways to take pictures 9
   ADD A SHUTTER BUTTON TO YOUR GALAXY CAMERA 10
      Remove the shutter button from your Galaxy Camera 10
   SETTING THE SHOOTING MODE 11
      Object Image Stabilization 11
      Night Portrait 11
CHAPTER 2 12
SAMSUNG GALAXY S23 CAMERA FEATURES YOU SHOULD TRY 12
   1. CAPTURE PHOTOS IN FULL 50MP RESOLUTION 12
   2. ENABLE SCENE OPTIMIZER 12
   3. INCREASE TIMER IN NIGHT MODE 13
   4. USE ASTROPHOTOGRAPHY MODE 14
   5. USE SINGLE TAKE 15
   6. CHANGE THE COLOR TONE FOR SELFIES 15
   7. USE AUTO FRAME FOR VIDEOS 16
CHAPTER 3 18
USING THE CAMERA APP ON GALAXY S23 SERIES MODELS 18
   OBJECT IMAGE STABILIZATION 18
   IMPORTANT NOTE: 10 XS TELEPHOTO IS AVAILABLE ONLY ON THE S23 ULTRA. 18
      Night Portrait 18
      Auto Framing 19
   ADVANCED AUTO FRAMING ON SAMSUNG GALAXY S23 SERIES 19
CHAPTER 4 22
USE PORTRAIT MODE OR LIVE FOCUS ON YOUR GALAXY SMARTPHONE 22

TAKE AMAZING PORTRAITS USING GALAXY PHONES 22

USE PORTRAIT VIDEO 22

CHAPTER 5 24

DIRECTOR VIEW AND DUAL RECORDING 24

RECORD MORE SIMULTANEOUSLY WITH DIRECTOR VIEW & DUAL RECORDING 24

CHAPTER 6 27

HOW TO MAKE USE OF SINGLE TAKE 27

USE SINGLE TAKE 27
    Record video 28
    Zoom-in mic 29
    Take paranoma on Samsung phone 29

CHAPTER 7 31

USE FOOD MODE TO CAPTURE FLAVOR 31

USING THE FOOD MODE 31
GOOD FOOD DESERVES FOOD MODE 31
ADJUST THE FOCUS TO CAPTURE DETAILS 32
GREAT PHOTOS IN ANY LIGHTING 32
IT IS PART OF THE PHOTOS HOLDING THE FOOD 32

CHAPTER 8 33

HOW TO USE PRO MODE OR PRO VIDEO MODE ON YOUR GALAXY PHONE PRO VIDEO 33

AVAILABLE OPTIONS 33

CHAPTER 9 35

NEW LEVEL OF SLOW MOTION WITH GALAXY PHONE SUPER SLOW MOTION 35

INTRODUCTION TO SUPER SLOW-MO 35
    What is Super Slow-Mo? 35
    Super Slow-Mo (Auto) 35
    Super Slow-Mo (Manual) 36
    Tips for Super Slow-Mo 36

CHAPTER 10 38

HOW TO USE HYPERLAPSE/TIMELAPSE 38

WHAT IS TIME-LAPSE? 38
HYPERLAPSE VS. TIMELAPSE PHOTOGRAPHY: WHAT'S THE DIFFERENCE? 38
THE BASIC TIMELAPSE 38
    Timelapse + Movement = Hyperlapse 39
    Choosing the Right 'Lapse 40

How to make a Timelapse on the Galaxy S23 .... *40*
Adjust Hyperlapse speed *41*
Activate or Deactivate a Timer *41*

CHAPTER 11 43

USING THE GALLERY APP ON A SMARTPHONE OR TABLET 43

HOW TO LOOK AT PICTURES 43
VIEWING AND EDITING PHOTOS AND VIDEOS 43
Move photos and videos to albums *44*
Delete photos and videos *45*
Create an album *45*
Group albums *45*
USE A GALLERY WIDGET 46
GALLERY SETTINGS 46
Create Stories *47*
Share photos and videos *47*

CHAPTER 12 49

USES OF AR ZONE IN S23 49

AR EMOJI CAMERA: 50
AR DOODLE: 50
AR EMOJI STUDIO: 51
MAKE A SHORT AR EMOJI VIDEO AND USE IT TO ADORN YOUR DEVICE: 51
CREATE A CONTACT PROFILE WITH AN AR EMOJI: 51
AR EMOJI STICKER: 51
DELETE AR EMOJI STICKERS: 52
USING AR EMOJI STICKERS IN CHATS: 52
DECO IMAGE: 52
USING DIRECTOR'S VIEW 52
Multi-camera standby *52*
Vlogger mode *53*
DIRECTOR'S VIEW: HOW TO SHOOT 53

CHAPTER 13 54

EDIT PHOTOS AND VIDEOS 54

FACE EFFECTS 54
OBJECT ERASER 54
SPOT COLOUR 55
STYLE 56
Colour mix *56*
VIDEO EDITING 57
ADDITIONAL TOOLS FOR EDITING PHOTOS/VIDEOS 59

SET A PHOTO OR VIDEO AS WALLPAPER	66
How to Set a Video as Your Lock Screen Wallpaper	*66*
Set a Video as Your Home Screen Wallpaper	*67*

CHAPTER 14 69

RECORD, EDIT, AND SHARE 8K VIDEO ON GALAXY PHONE 69

8K VIDEO RECORDING AND EDITING	69
SHARE 8K VIDEO	71

CHAPTER 15 72

CUSTOMIZE THEMES AND ICONS 72

DOWNLOAD THEME	72
Change theme	*72*
DOWNLOAD ICON	72
CHANGE ICON	73
Remove theme	*74*
Delete icon	*74*
Restore purchased themes	*74*

CHAPTER 16 76

VARIOUS CAMERA MODES & HOW TO USE THEM 76

WHERE CAN I FIND THE DIFFERENT CAMERA MODES AND CAN I DOWNLOAD MORE?	76
AR (AUGMENTED REALITY) EMOJI	76
Fast Motion/Hyperlapse	*76*
Flaw detection	*77*
Live Focus/Portrait Mode	*78*
Scene Optimizer	*78*
Telephone Mode	*79*

CHAPTER 17 80

USING SAMSUNG EXPERT RAW TO IMPROVE YOUR PHOTOGRAPHY 80

WHAT IS SAMSUNG EXPERT RAW?	80
SAMSUNG CAMERA APP VS. EXPERT RAW	80
What is Samsung Expert Raw?	*80*
HOW TO GET SAMSUNG EXPERT RAW ON YOUR PHONE	81
EXPERT RAW VS. A STANDARD CAMERA APP	81
How to use Samsung Expert RAW	*83*
Edit and Take Pictures with Samsung Expert RAW Using Samsung Expert RAW	*85*
How to Edit RAW Images for Expert RAW	*85*

CHAPTER 18 86

SAMSUNG CAMERA ASSISTANT APP 86

What is the Samsung Camera Assistant app? 86
How to download the Samsung Camera Assistant app 88

CHAPTER 19 90

POST PRODUCTION- EDIT VIDEOS WITH THE INSHOT APP 90

Download the Inshot App 90
Add photos and videos to your video 90
Import other photos and videos 91
Arrange clips 91
    Increase the timeline 92
    Delete clips 92
    Add effects or edits to all video clips 92
    Resize video 92
    Change Background 93
    Crop Video 93
    Add audio from video 93
    Extract audio from an existing video 94
    Extract Audio from Current Video 94
Removing background noise from your videos 94
    Add Sticker 95
    Customize text 95
    Add filters and effects 95
    Add a transition 96
    Add multiple videos in one frame 96
    Cut, trim, and split video 96
    Speed, Rotate, and Flip 96
    Freeze Frame 97
    Removing watermark from videos 97
    Save video 97

CHAPTER 20 98

PHONE PHOTOGRAPHY BASICS: HOW TO TAKE GOOD PHOTOS WITH YOUR MOBILE DEVICE 98

Use grid lines to balance your shots 98
    Set your camera's focus. 99
Use HDR mode. 99
Use natural light. 100
    Adjust the camera focus 101
    Frame and balance your shots 101
    Play with different perspectives 102
Use a Tripod 102
    Make sure your camera lens is clean 103
    Keep your distance 103

Check the lighting 103
USE NEGATIVE SPACES 103
   Understanding negative space in photography 104
   Positive and negative space: What's the difference? 104
   Why is it called "negative space"? 104
   What is an example of negative space? 105
HOW DOES NEGATIVE SPACE AFFECT PHOTOGRAPHY? 105
   Why is negative space important? 106
   How to create negative space in your photos 106
   Does negative space have to be black or white? 109
FIND DIFFERENT POINTS OF VIEW 110
   Experiment with Reflections 110
   Use Guidelines 110
   Look for symmetry 111
PAY ATTENTION TO THE REPEATING PATTERN 112
EXPERIMENT WITH COLOUR BLOCKING 113
   Don't Zoom in 113
   Capture small details. 114
USE FLASH ONLY DURING THE DAY 114
ADJUST THE EXPOSURE MANUALLY IN THE CAMERA APP 114
   Create abstracts. 115
CAPTURING CANDIDS 116
   Be Eccentric. 116
   Force them to laugh 116
   Clean the cell phone lens 117
   Attach an external lens. 117
EDIT YOUR IMAGES 118
SHOOT BETTER PICTURES 118
CONCLUSION 119

INDEX 120

INTRODUCTION

The Galaxy S23 series is still making waves, and even though they do not exactly live up to the built-up hype, the new camera upgrades still play a big part in this year's lineup. On paper, the S23 and S23 Plus' 12-megapixel camera seems to be an upgrade over its predecessors' 10-megapixel selfie cameras. The S22 boasts a selfie camera with a resolution of 40 megapixels, so at first glance; the Ultra's new front camera can seem inferior. Nevertheless, having fewer megapixels isn't necessarily a terrible thing. Samsung worked to enhance the new selfie camera's capacity to identify subjects from their surroundings with clarity.

The new camera now supports Super HDR, which enhances color, contrast, and brightness for footage captured at 4K 60fps. Speaking of video, the Galaxy S23 series's rear cameras can all capture video at an improved 8K 30 frames per second, compared to the 8K 24 frames per second of the Galaxy S22 lineup. Many applications including TikTok, Instagram, and YouTube offer frame rates at 30 fps. The 8K 30fps setting isn't meant to be used often.

But, 8K could be handy if you want to view your films on a bigger screen that supports 8K or if you want to capture footage for a movie, as Samsung constantly stated during their introduction. Also, it's crucial to remember that 8K movies sometimes need more storage than those captured in 4K or HD. Samsung improved the field of view on the Galaxy S23 Ultra's camera when recording in 8K, which is wonderful since the crop was pronounced on older Galaxy S phones that supported 8K.

The triple rear cameras on the Galaxy S23 and S23 Plus are almost similar to those on its predecessors from a hardware perspective, but Samsung claims to have enhanced features like dynamic range and glare reduction. The Samsung S23 Ultra clearly displayed these adjustments, even if we haven't tried the Galaxy S23 or S23 Plus. Because Samsung removed the camera hump, the cameras on the S23 and S23 Plus now mirror those on the S23 Ultra.

So, what does each camera do?

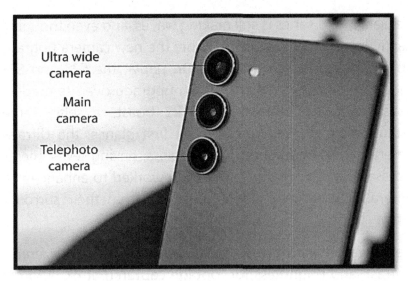

Let's start with the Main camera, which has a wide-angle lens and is positioned in the middle of the other two cameras. You'll use this as your daily driver. While the main camera provides a 50-megapixel shooting option, full-resolution images must be taken in well-lit settings for the best clarity.

While you may have 50 million pixels to work with, phone sensors and their pixels are very tiny and don't absorb as much light as older DSLRs or modern mirrorless cameras. This increases picture noise and necessitates the employment of extra noise-reduction processing.

Instead, the camera software on Samsung phones defaults to 12-megapixel images, which merge many smaller pixels into one bigger pixel. In medium- and low-light circumstances, the procedure is known as "**pixel binning**," because it produces less picture noise and higher-quality photographs (think inside a dark restaurant).

The 12-megapixel ultra-wide camera, which is similar to the one on its predecessor, is next in the camera array. Pinch in on your screen to switch to this camera's 120-degree field of view if you want to capture more of your surroundings. The extra wide lens is perfect for filming vistas, and the exaggerated appearance allows for recordings that seem dramatic. It's a great camera to use for slow-motion photography. The 10-megapixel telephoto camera with a 3x optical zoom lens is the last one, located at the bottom of the array. Telephoto lenses provide improved imaging of distant objects, backdrops, and subjects. By zooming in, you can assist eliminate unwanted objects from your image. You'll also take portrait-mode photos with this camera.

Naturally, you can utilize Single Shot mode to capture pictures with each of the three back cameras at the same time.

Galaxy S23 Ultra's four rear cameras include a 200-megapixel main camera

The Galaxy S23 Ultra, Samsung's high-end flagship model, had the most significant camera enhancements. The Ultra has a quadruple back camera system in contrast to the other two S23 series phones. The Galaxy S23 Ultra's main camera has a 200-megapixel sensor, which is a substantial improvement over the Galaxy S22 Ultra's. The main attraction is this camera. Generally speaking, you won't need to shoot at the highest quality unless you want to publish your pictures at enormous proportions. Similar to the S23 and S23 Plus, the Ultra's main camera employs pixel binning and captures 12-megapixel photographs by default. Simply said, the Ultra has more group-able pixels, which results in images that appear better, are brighter, and have less image noise, even in low light conditions.

Super Quad Pixel, an enhanced focusing technique that employs 2x2 pixel groups to enable the camera's focus lock onto elements like vistas or tree trunks even in low light, is another feature of the upgraded sensor. The **Expert Raw app**, which the S23 Ultra also supports, enables you to take pictures using Samsung's computational methods and save them as raw files to preserve more image data and a wider dynamic range. While raw files are often bigger than **JPEG** files, they are better for altering photos since they include more picture data and settings. All of the cameras on the S23 Ultra are compatible with **Samsung's Expert Raw** software, and after installation, the native camera app has access to the app's features.

Instead of the single telephoto camera present in the S23 and S23 Plus, there are two telephoto cameras and a 12-megapixel ultra-wide camera in addition to the primary camera. In contrast to the second telephoto lens, which has a 10x optical zoom, the first one has a 3x optical zoom. The second telephoto camera has a 100x digital zoom as well, but as you zoom in, the photos get noisier. The digital zoom on the 10x telephoto could provide respectable images at magnifications of 25 to 30 times, assuming it is anything like prior Galaxy Ultra phones.

CHAPTER 1

MASTERING THE S23 CAMERA APP

What are the 4 ways to launch the Galaxy S23 camera app?

The camera can be launched in three ways: via the **Lock Screen, the Power button,** or the **Apps Screen.**

Step 1: Through the Lock Screen

- To use the camera, tap the camera symbol in the bottom right corner of the screen and slide up.

(NB: Please note that when you launch the Camera program from a locked screen or when the screen is turned off and you have specified a locking mechanism, certain camera functionalities are not accessible (PIN, scheme, etc.).

Step 2: How to Use the Power Button

When **"Quick Launch"** is enabled, you can launch the camera by pressing the Power button twice on your phone.

- Press the Power button twice to start your Galaxy Camera.

To use Quick Launch, follow these steps:

- Start the camera.
- Select the Settings option.
- Scroll down and press the **"Quick Launch"** option to enable it.

Another possibility:

- To access advanced features, go to **"Settings"** and then **"Advanced Features."**
- Tap **"Side key"**.
- Toggle **"Double press"** on the switch, then choose **"Quick launch camera."**

Step 3: Using the Apps menu

- To access your applications, swipe up or down on the Home screen, then touch the **"Camera"** app.

New Features of the S23 series Camera app

Main features of the camera app

Night portrait and Night selfie

Your photographs will come out with stunningly high quality and sharp details thanks to the Nightography capabilities included in the Galaxy S23 series.

1. First, access the **Camera** app and launch it, then slide right until you reach **MORE** and press it.

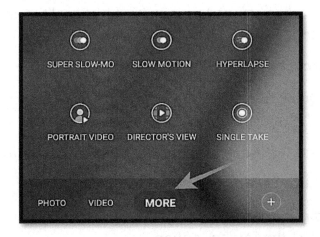

2. Choose **NIGHT**, and then align your picture as desired. You can zoom in and out by squeezing the screen with your fingers, or by selecting one of the available choices at the bottom of the screen, such as 3x or 10x. Alternatively, you can swipe your finger from left to right across the screen to zoom in and out.
3. Tap **Capture**.
4. Alternatively, you can press the symbol that looks like a camera switch to switch to the front camera. To snap a selfie, use the **Capture** button.

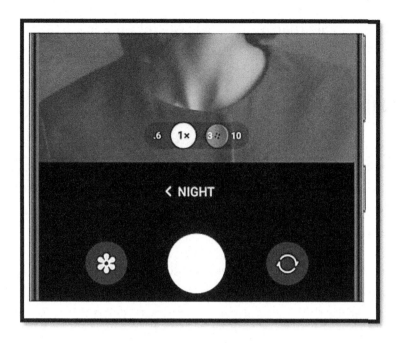

Night video and Night selfie video

Using a mobile device from the Galaxy S23 series, you may capture movies using cutting-edge nightography features. While using Night movie mode, the automated super steady feature will allow you to shoot wide photos that are completely smooth even as you're moving about.

If you and your pals like to shoot some selfies together, you may take advantage of the Night selfie films.

1. To start recording, open the Camera app and click the **VIDEO** icon.
2. Tap the Night shot icon, which resembles a crescent moon, to start **Night shoot**. To begin capturing video, press the **Record** button next.
3. You can enlarge or reduce the size of the image by pinching the screen with your fingers or by selecting one of the options at the bottom of the image, such as 3 xs or 10 xs. By moving your finger over the screen from left to right, you can also zoom in and out.
4. You will get a reminder to keep your phone steady while filming. Use the Stop button to end the recording.

5. As an alternative, you can switch to the front camera by pressing the icon that resembles a camera switch. To record a selfie video, tap Record.

Additional features

Some of your preferred photographs and GIFs will look better thanks to the inbuilt AI Picture Enhancer on the Galaxy S23. Its artificial intelligence will increase resolution and clarity by reducing background noise, making your portraits brighter and your movement shots seem more distinct.

When looking through your memories in the Gallery app, you may choose to utilize the function that allows you to write fresh tales. Stories that an algorithm will suggest and develop on its own will be built on the base of your images and videos. Afterwards, you may utilize specially crafted Spotify playlists to change the story's tone using the music playing in the background.

The Expert RAW software, which can be downloaded from the Galaxy Store, gives users the ability to take photographs of professional quality on their Galaxy S23 series devices.

Different ways to take pictures

On your S23 Series, you can snap a shot by pressing the Volume key, speaking into the phone, touching a shutter button on the screen, or facing your palm to the screen.

1. Start the camera.
2. Select the **Settings option**.
3. Select **"Shooting methods"** from the menu.

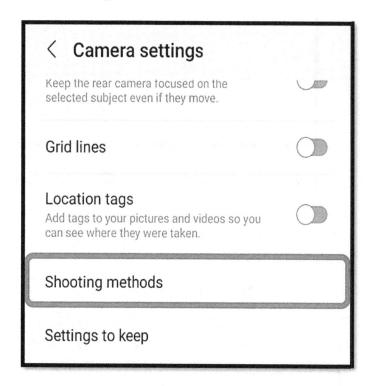

4. From the various choices, choose your chosen settings.

Other options:

- **Press the Volume key** to choose the setting you want to manage with the Volume key, which includes **"Take or record video,"** "Zoom," and "Control the System volume."

- If you wish to snap a photo by speaking certain phrases like "**Smile**" or "**Shoot**," turn on **Voice Command**.
- **Floating Shutter Button:** Place another shutter button on the screen to make it easier to push; once activated, touch and hold the shutter button, and then drag it to the desired area on the screen.

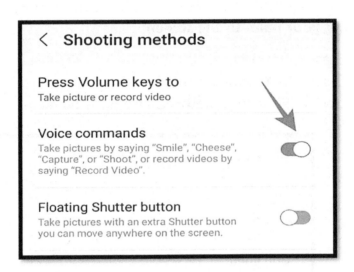

Add a shutter button to your Galaxy Camera

- Drag it back to the original shutter position to delete it, or hit and hold the second shutter button again, and then tap the **Minus symbol**.

Remove the shutter button from your Galaxy Camera

- **Show palm:** Choose this option if you want to shoot a selfie with your palm facing the screen of your smartphone.

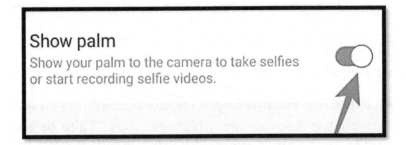

Setting the Shooting mode

Object Image Stabilization

The S23 series' Object Image Stabilization has been enhanced to significantly eliminate blurriness and unexpected movements during video recording.

Your whole group will remain in the frame for a seamless and clear movie!

1. Open and go to the Camera app, then hit **VIDEO**.
2. Zoom to 1x, 3 xs, or 10 xs.
Important note: 10 xs Telephoto is available only on the S23 Ultra.
3. Finally, hit **Record** to begin recording. While you're recording, **Object Image Stabilization** will operate automatically.
4. When completed, tap **Stop**.

Night Portrait

Note: Night Portrait is not feasible while using a 3x zoom. You can take stunning photos in low light with the Night Portrait feature on the S23 series. You can also take pictures outside after dark!

For nighttime photography, you can use both the front and rear lenses.

1. In the Camera app, choose **PORTRAIT**, and then click **OK**.
2. The Night shot icon, which looks like a crescent moon, displays in the bottom right corner of the viewfinder whenever the lens sensors determine that you are in a dark area.
3. The **Night shot** sign will glow gray when it is off and yellow when it is on. If required, activate it by clicking the **Night shot** icon.
4. While still in control of your phone, click **Capture**.

CHAPTER 2
SAMSUNG GALAXY S23 CAMERA FEATURES YOU SHOULD TRY

1. CAPTURE PHOTOS IN FULL 50MP RESOLUTION

The main camera of the Samsung Galaxy S23 and Galaxy S23 Plus features a 50MP primary sensor. But, by default, it will record photographs at a pixel-binned resolution of 12 megapixels. Having said that, you are also able to take pictures with a resolution of up to 50 megapixels.

To do this, launch the camera and go to **Picture mode**. Then, choose the aspect ratio icon that is located at the top of the screen. Make your selection using the 50MP mode found here.

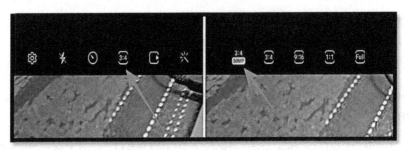

And that's it. Now, every single shot you take will be saved at a full resolution of 50MP. Please bear in mind that photos with the full 50 MP qualities are much bigger. Because of this, we strongly advise restoring to the previous configuration; otherwise, you run the danger of running out of available storage space.

2. ENABLE SCENE OPTIMIZER

From out of the box, the camera on the Galaxy S23 is capable of capturing beautiful shots. On the other hand, to get results with a greater sense of vibrancy, you may need to manually edit the photographs, which is a laborious process in and of itself. To our relief, this is where artificial intelligence enters the picture (no pun intended).

The camera software that comes standard on the Samsung Galaxy S23 has a Scene Optimizer function that uses AI to improve the quality of your photographs. The final product is colourful, and the sensor can take pictures that are suitable for sharing on social media.

Launch the **camera app** in photo mode, and then hit the setting icon located at the very top of the screen. Doing so will activate the scene optimizer. Activate the toggle that is located next to the Scene Optimizer from this screen.

3. INCREASE TIMER IN NIGHT MODE

The Galaxy S23 series comes with a night mode that can help you shoot amazing photographs even when there is little available light. On the other hand, the smartphone analyses the environment and adjusts the shutter speed of the camera appropriately.

Having said that, if you want the greatest results possible, it is advised that you leave the shutter open for a little longer, enabling the maximum amount of light to strike the camera sensor.

This can be done by keeping the shutter open for a bit longer.

- Launch the camera app, then slide left on the ribbon located at the bottom of the screen until you reach the tab labelled "**More**." From here, tap on **night mode**.

- A timer symbol should have shown in the bottom right-hand corner at this point. You should then choose **Max** from the menu that appears once you press it.

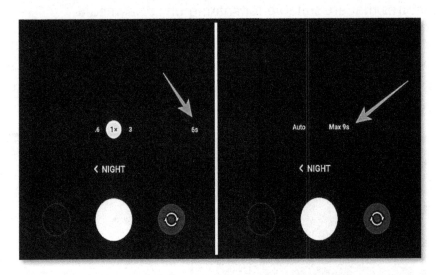

That brings us to the end! The shutter on the camera will remain open for a much longer period now. All that is required of you is to maintain a steady hand on the phone until the photo has been completely taken.

4. USE ASTROPHOTOGRAPHY MODE

When it comes to night mode, the majority of users like to take pictures of the night sky complete with all of the stars. On the other hand, if you use the camera on the Samsung Galaxy S23, you'll have an even higher chance of capturing the beauty of the night sky thanks to the astrophotography option.

To make use of it, launch the camera app and then go to the tab labelled "**More**." Here, tap on **Expert RAW.**

To activate the mode, all that is required of you at this point is to choose the astrophoto icon located at the very top of the screen. You can choose the length of time that the Astrophoto mode captures from four to ten minutes, and you can even display star trails that are specific to your region.

5. USE SINGLE TAKE

It wouldn't be inaccurate to say that Single Take is one of the greatest photography capabilities available on the Samsung Galaxy S23. It starts by taking a video, which is then followed by the generation of additional still images and moving images automatically.

Launch the camera app and go to the tab labelled "**More**" to activate the **Single Take feature**. Tap the **Single Take option**. In addition, you can tailor the kinds of outcomes that are produced by Single Take. To accomplish so, just touch on the **customize symbol** that is located in the upper-right-hand corner of the screen. Now, all you have to do is touch on the different styles to pick or deselect them according to your preferences. After you are finished, all you need to do is make sure you touch the Ok button to preserve your selections. And, just like that, you can now enjoy using the Single Take mode on your Samsung Galaxy S23 camera.

6. CHANGE THE COLOR TONE FOR SELFIES

The front-facing camera on the Samsung Galaxy S23 has a resolution of 12 megapixels, making it ideal for taking selfies. The images already have a high level of detail, but you can customize the colour tone to make it more or less vivid if you choose. To do this, launch the camera app with the Photo mode selected, and then, to switch to the Selfie mode, press on the flip symbol that is located next to the shutter button.

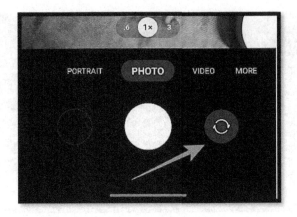

Then, choose the **Magic wand** symbol located in the upper-right-hand area of the screen. After that, choose **Color tone** from the list of available options that appears.

7. USE AUTO FRAME FOR VIDEOS

Turning on the Auto Frame option for movies is just another thing you can do to improve your camera's overall performance. After your topic has been highlighted using this unique technique for the Galaxy S23 camera, you can be certain that it will remain in the centre of the picture at all times. When the camera detects that the subject is moving away from the centre of the picture, it will zoom in to follow it.

Launch the camera app and choose the Video shooting mode before making use of the Auto Frame feature. Now, touch the symbol that looks like a frame in the bottom-right corner of the screen.

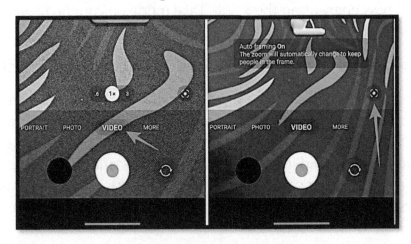

You will get a notice letting you know that Auto framing has been turned on. Just touch on the topic that you want to bring more attention to and stay in the spotlight. At this point, the camera will automatically zoom in closer to the subject to place it in the middle of the frame.

If activated, the subject will always stay in the centre of the picture, regardless of the movement of the camera or where you are standing. It is important to keep in mind, however, that when the Auto Frame function is used, the Super Steady video mode is turned off automatically.

CHAPTER 3
USING THE CAMERA APP ON GALAXY S23 SERIES MODELS

Object image stabilization

The Object Image Stabilization of the S23 series has been dramatically improved, and as a result, blurriness and unexpected movements that occur during video recording have been much reduced. Your whole party will stay inside the confines of the frame to ensure a smooth and unbroken video!

1. Launch the Camera app, and then choose VIDEO from the menu that appears.
2. Zoom to 1x, 3 xs, or 10 xs.

Important note: 10 xs Telephoto is available only on the S23 Ultra.

3. When you are ready to start recording, click the **Record** button. Object Image Stabilization will work on its own without any input from you while you are recording.
4. When it's done, touch the **Stop** button.

Night Portrait

Note: Night Portrait is not feasible while using a 3x zoom. Using the Night Portrait mode on the S23 series, you can shoot excellent images even when there is little available light. You can even shoot photographs outdoors after dark if you want to!

Both the front and the back lenses can be used for taking photographs throughout the night.

1. Launch the Camera app, choose **PORTRAIT** from the shooting mode menu, and then tap the OK button.
2. The symbol for night shots, which resembles a crescent moon and can be seen in the lower right-hand corner of the viewfinder,

appears anytime the lens sensors detect that you are in a dimly lit environment.
3. While turned off, the Night shot sign will emit a gray light; when activated, it will emit a yellow glow. If you need to use it, activate it by clicking the symbol that looks like a night camera.
4. While you are still in charge of your phone, choose the **Capture** option.

Auto Framing

Advanced Auto Framing is one of those features that make use of computational techniques to assist you to capture the finest image possible, even if you are just a beginner photographer. This function is available in more advanced versions of the software. Let's get more information on it, figure out how it operates, and determine what kinds of situations it is most helpful in.

Advanced Auto Framing on Samsung Galaxy S23 Series

The vast majority of individuals can take a picture with their smartphone by aiming the device toward the topic they want to photograph and then pressing the shutter button. Even if today's smartphones were designed to be used in exactly this manner, there are still methods that can enhance your photographic skills.

This comprises some guidelines that deal with the arrangement of the elements in the picture. Your photograph's composition is mostly determined by the elements that are visible inside the frame of the photo.

You may have noticed that the camera app on your phone provides an option to activate grid lines or diagonal lines while taking pictures. You can even be familiar with the phrase "rule of thirds," which is often used by professional photographers. These are the instruments that assist in the creation of a strong composition, which ultimately leads to the capturing of a nice photograph.

On the other hand, the everyday person isn't going to know or care much about these regulations. The main objective is to take excellent images and movies without worrying about the composition of the shot or where on the grid the subject of the photo or video should be placed. To address this same issue, Samsung developed something called **Advanced Auto Framing.**

The Advanced Auto Framing feature will automatically calculate the location of the subject you are photographing as well as detect the subject itself. The smartphone is then capable of adjusting the composition of the shot in response to the location of the subject. To put it more simply, while you are capturing a video of a human subject, the camera will zoom in or out to maintain the subject's position inside the frame.

This function is quite similar to one that was introduced by Apple on the iPad and called "**Centre Stage**." The Advanced Auto Framing feature, which is available on the Galaxy S23 series of phones, can be used when shooting videos using the rear cameras. However, that function is only available while making video calls.

Also, this function will optimize the focus points with the location of your topic. When you are taking a picture of someone who is a little bit farther away from you, the camera will zoom in closer to the subject and also change its focus toward that person. Up until this point, we'd seen smartphone cameras adjust the scene per the subject being captured. This meant that many aspects of the image, such as the colours, saturation, and contrast, were modified automatically depending on the sort of photo that you were shooting.

With its Advanced Auto Framing feature, Samsung is taking things to the next level by automatically cropping and composing your shots for you depending on the location of the subject in the frame. Your subject will be locked into focus by the phone, and the zoom range will be automatically adjusted to either go closer to the topic or move further away from it, depending on your preference. While you are filming a video of a person, the phone will automatically zoom in on the face and lock the focus there to produce an effect similar to a portrait.

According to Samsung, its Advanced Auto Framing feature can identify up to ten objects and adjusts both the focus and the composition of the photo appropriately. Since the phone changes the framing on its own without the user having to make any further efforts, this is an excellent feature for those who just point and shoot their photos. This describes the majority of people, except professionals. It is important to keep in mind, however, that the Advanced Auto Framing feature is only active while the camera is recording movies and not when it is collecting still photographs.

CHAPTER 4

USE PORTRAIT MODE OR LIVE FOCUS ON YOUR GALAXY SMARTPHONE

Take amazing portraits using Galaxy phones

- Launch the Camera app
- Swipe to **MORE**
- Tap on **PORTRAIT**
- Tap on the **Effect** icon
- Choose the preferred background effect
- Adjust background effect intensity
- When you are ready to take your photo tap on the capture button

Use Portrait video

Launch the Camera app, and then choose **MORE** from the menu. Touch either the **LIVE FOCUS VIDEO** or the **PORTRAIT VIDEO** option, and then tap the circle located in the view finder's bottom right corner. There are four different options available, and the slider can be used to make adjustments to each one.

- **Blur**: This will blur the backdrop surrounding the topic that you are shooting to give it a more mysterious appearance.
- **Big circle**: Creates a concentrated circle around your topic while drastically blurring the backdrop. This mode is useful for bringing attention to certain details.

- **Colorpoint:** Changes the sharpness of the colours directly around your subject, so everything else becomes black and white.
- **Glitch**: This will provide an effect in the backdrop that looks like multicolored static.

CHAPTER 5
DIRECTOR VIEW AND DUAL RECORDING

Record more simultaneously with Director View & Dual Recording

You can use Director's View by itself (without the usage of the selfie camera) or by pairing it with Dual recording, which enables you to record with both the back camera and the selfie camera at the same time.

You also can swap between the lenses of the back camera while you are in the Director's View.

1. Open the Camera app.
2. After tapping **MORE**, choose **DIRECTOR'S VIEW** from the menu that appears.
3. At the very bottom of the screen, you will see a selection of several lens selections. Tap the arrow that is pointing upwards towards the bottom of the screen if you do not see these available choices.
4. After you have begun recording, you can still move between the various camera lenses by tapping the available selections. As an example, you can immediately swap between the ultra-wide lens and the telephoto lens. Swiping your finger up or down on the screen allows you to switch between the front-facing camera and the back camera.
5. To switch to dual recording mode, hit the **rectangle** symbol that is located in the top right corner of the screen. Depending on the mode that's now active, it will have a look that's just a little bit different.

6. **From this screen, choose the recording option that you want to use:**
    - To watch yourself in real-time while you record, tap the button labelled "**Picture-in-picture**," which will cause a little window to emerge in one of the screen's corners.
    - Choose the **Split icon** from the toolbar to show the viewfinder on top of the camera and the front-facing camera on the bottom. You will get a comprehensive picture of both the subject matter of the tape and yourself.
    - Touch the **Single symbol** to make the viewfinder of the camera the only visible element. That's another way of saying that this will switch off dual recording as well as the selfie camera.
7. You can record the video of the selfie front view and the main video of the rear-view as two different files! To do this, press the **Download** symbol (it looks like a box with an arrow pointing down inside of it) that is placed at the top of the screen before you begin recording. When it is configured to download each movie in its separate session, the icon will display a pair of checkboxes. If you press on this symbol, you can save the video in its previewed state.

    Please take note that this particular configuration option is not presently accessible on any other device save those in the S22 and S23 series.

8. When you have selected the parameters that you want, hit the Record button to start recording a video.
9. You can switch between the lenses of the back camera even when it is shooting a video. But, once you begin recording a video, you won't be able to modify the setting for the Dual recording function, so be sure you choose one before you begin.
Remember that turning off Dual recording requires switching from the main camera to the front-facing camera while the recording is in progress.
10. To temporarily stop recording, tap the **pause** symbol. You can keep recording by pressing the symbol that looks like a record button.
11. After you are done, touch the **stop sign icon**. The video will be stored in the app called Gallery after it is finished.

CHAPTER 6
HOW TO MAKE USE OF SINGLE TAKE

Use Single Take

Single Take allows you to take wide-angle, close-up, and video images. In Single Take mode, the zoom feature is disabled.

Step 1: Open the **Camera app** first. Navigate to the "**MORE**" menu and select **SINGLE TAKE**.

Step 2: To get the best photo, press the shutter button and pan about. Any scene's finest image and clips will be captured automatically by the camera.

Step 3: When you're done, touch the thumbnail preview. For the scene you photographed, you will receive optimum results.

Simply slide the icon higher to see more results. To save the results individually, press Select and check the things you want, and then hit the down arrow symbol.

The kind of outcomes that Single Take produces can be changed. Just touch on the customize symbol in the top-right corner to accomplish that. Just press on the styles again to pick or deselect them as you like.

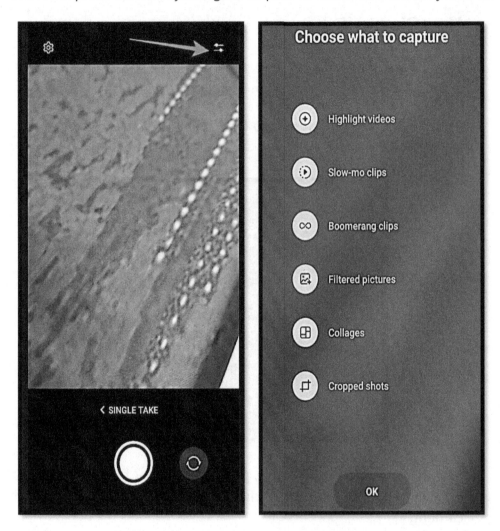

Once done, just make sure to tap on Ok to save your preferences. And, just like that, you can now enjoy using the Single Take mode on your Samsung Galaxy S23 camera.

Record video

- From the Home screen, swipe up from the centre of the display to access the app screen.

- Tap the **Camera icon**.
    - If necessary, tap **Video** located above the camera swap icon.
- Aim then tap the Record icon to begin recording.
- When finished, tap the **Stop icon** to discontinue recording.
- Tap the image preview located in the lower-left to view the video.
- Tap the **Share icon** (at the bottom).
    - If necessary, tap the screen to display the options.
- Select one of the available options (e.g., Bluetooth, Cloud, Email, Gmail, Messages, YouTube, etc.).
    - Depending on the apps installed, the options presented may vary.
- Enter any additional info required to send or share the video.
    - Depending upon the share option selected the remaining steps to send or share may vary.

Zoom-in mic

Launch the camera app, hit the Settings button, scroll down, and pick Enhanced recording from the menu that appears. Now, turn on the Zoom-in mic option by toggling the switch.

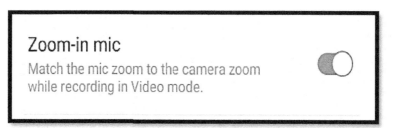

If enabled, a microphone symbol will appear anytime you zoom in on a subject while the camera is in video mode. This indicator indicates the degree to which the audio is being zoomed in.

Take paranoma on Samsung phone

- From the home screen, choose Apps or swipe up to access your apps
- Tap Camera

- Choose Panorama
- Choose Mode or swipe across the screen to select panorama mode.
- Press the capture button to start taking your photo
- The screen will show an alignment box to help you keep the scene aligned.
- Slowly move the device in one direction
- When you touch the stop button or you reach the maximum range your device will make the necessary adjustments and stitch the images together to form one complete panoramic photo
- To view the captured Panorama, choose the preview thumbnail.

CHAPTER 7
USE FOOD MODE TO CAPTURE FLAVOR

Using the Food Mode

- From the home screen choose Apps or swipe up to access your apps.
- Choose Camera.
- Choose MODE or swipe right on the screen to access the mode menu.
- Choose Food.
- Press and hold the circular frame, then place it over the subject (The area outside the circle will be blurred). To resize the circular frame, drag a corner of the frame until happy.
- Choose the Capture button to take your picture.

Good food deserves Food mode

When we snap a selfie with our smartphone, it is typical practice for most of us to search for the optimal shooting perspective. Nevertheless, we do not just do this when we are taking pictures of people's faces; we also do it when we are taking pictures of our meals, a practice that has become increasingly prevalent, particularly when we share the details of our everyday lives on social networking sites. When seen via the camera of the Galaxy S23 5G, any dish will have an amazing appearance.

Just launch the camera app on your Samsung Galaxy mobile, choose "**More**" from the available options, and then select "**Food**" from the menu that appears. This will allow you to record any kind of food. With this mode, you can catch the finer characteristics of a dish, such as those seen in upscale eateries, such as ice cream on a warm day, bubbles in a glass of soda, or that upscale burger in a quick-service restaurant.

Take your food photography to the next level with these incredible pointers for using the Galaxy S23 5G cameras to their full potential.

Adjust the focus to capture details

The Galaxy S23 5G's Food mode is equipped with an automated focus adjustment that kicks in as soon as the camera is brought into proximity to the subject of the shot. But, you should experiment with this function as much as possible, zooming in or out to change the level of depth of detail in the meal. You can keep the item on its side, and by blurring the backdrop, you can make the meal or drink stand out even more in the photograph.

Great photos in any lighting

You will find that each eatery, whether a restaurant, bar, or cafeteria, often provides its illumination, which is not even close to being the same in any of these settings. In contrast to the brighter lighting that could be seen at a chain fast food restaurant, the atmosphere in a smaller, more cosy eatery tends to be darker and cosier.

Make use of the **Nightography feature** of the Galaxy S23 5G if you are in an area with little or no illumination. This ability will allow you to capture detail and clarity regardless of the amount of light present.

When it's time to snap images, expand your horizons by using the 200MP lens on the Galaxy S23 Ultra 5G to capture more than one thing at a moment. For example, the glasses of drink next to a lovely dish of pasta at your favourite Italian restaurant are perfect examples of this.

In addition, if it is a treat like ice cream with chocolate syrup, you should position the container next to the main course so that guests can easily reach it. Focus on the composition to produce eye-catching photographs that can spread quickly through social networks.

It is part of the photos holding the food

Thanks to the front cameras of the S23 5G, which can also shoot photographs and movies with Nightography, you not only have the ability to include a variety of things in the shot, but you also can appear in the photo regardless of the ambient light.

CHAPTER 8

HOW TO USE PRO MODE OR PRO VIDEO MODE ON YOUR GALAXY PHONE Pro Video

1. Open the app that you use to take pictures.
2. From the selection of shooting modes, choose MORE PRO or PRO VIDEO to change the mode.
3. Pick the choices you want, tweak the settings, and change them to your liking after you've done so.

Available options

- **ISO**: Pick an ISO value. This adjusts how sensitive the camera is to light. Low values are assigned to things that are either immobile or well-lit. Greater values are assigned to things that are moving quickly or have a low level of illumination. But, higher ISO settings might cause noise in the images and videos that you capture.
- **Aperture & Shutter Speed**: Change the aperture and the shutter speed to get the desired effect. Since a slower shutter speed lets in more light, the resulting image or video will be more brightly lit. This is perfect for taking photographs or movies at night, as well as images or videos of the landscape during the day. A faster shutter speed lets in less light than a slower one. This works well for taking pictures or movies of things that are moving quickly.
- **Exposure**: Adjust the exposure value. The amount of light that reaches the sensor of the camera is determined by this. Use a greater exposure setting while working in low-light conditions.
- **Manual Focus:** Change the focus mode. To switch to autofocus mode, tap **MANUAL**.
- **White Balance**: Ensure that the photographs you capture have a colour range that is accurate by selecting the right white balance. You have control over the warmth of the colours.
- **Standard:** Adjust the colour tone.

- Remember that if you choose to manually adjust the shutter speed, you will not be able to choose AUTO for the ISO setting nor will you be able to modify the exposure value. The shutter speed setting will cause the exposure value to vary, and those changes will be shown on the screen.

CHAPTER 9

NEW LEVEL OF SLOW MOTION WITH GALAXY PHONE SUPER SLOW MOTION

Introduction to Super Slow-Mo

Your phone has a feature called Super Slow-Mo that enables you to capture films in slow motion, turning all of your favourite moments into something more theatrical. You can relive the event by slowing down the action in Super Slow-Mo Mode, whether it's you going up for a slam dunk on the basketball court or your kids running in the sprinkler.

Note: Super Slow-Mo is only available on select phones.

What is Super Slow-Mo?

With the help of an upgraded speed sensor on your phone, the Super Slow-Mo app enables you to take photos and videos at an astounding rate of 960 frames per second. While using Super Slow-Mo on a Galaxy S9 or earlier model, you can only record for 0.2 or 0.4 seconds at a time in slow motion. However, with a Galaxy S10 or later model, you can record for either 0.4 or 0.8 seconds at a time.

Please be aware that Super Slow-Mo only works with HD resolution. You are only allowed 20 shots per video.

Super Slow-Mo (Auto)

Use the Super Slow-Mo Auto option if you want the slow motion to look as good as it possibly can. When the camera is in this mode, it will automatically detect any motion and then begin to slow down. In addition to that, it enables you to include many instances of slow motion into a single film.

Tap the **MORE** buttons inside the Camera app, and then hit the **Super SLOW-MO** option. Finally, make sure that **Auto mode** is turned on by tapping the emblem that looks like an automobile. It seems to be three smaller circles contained inside a larger square. Tap the **Record** button when you are ready. Keep your phone still for the motion detection to begin working. If your camera determines that there is motion inside the square that is shown, it will immediately begin recording in super slow motion.

Super Slow-Mo (Manual)

With the version called Super Slow-Mo Manual, you can trigger slow motion on your own. If you make advantage of this feature, each movie will only include a single instance of the slow-motion effect.

Tap the **MORE** buttons inside the Camera app, and then hit the **SUPER SLOW-MO** option. Next, check to see that the **Auto mode** is not active. The motion detection symbol will appear as a gray square when the feature is disabled. It seems to be three smaller circles contained inside a larger square.

Tap the **Record** button when you are ready. Keep your phone still and record everything that's happening. After a few seconds, the recording on your phone will pause, and it will then generate a slow-motion movie automatically.

Tips for Super Slow-Mo

While making slow-motion films, even though Super Slow-Mo is an extremely sophisticated technique, there are still a few things that you will need to keep in mind.

Check out the following suggestions if you want your Super Slow-Mo videos to turn out the best:

- Be sure there are no moving things in the on-screen square (other than the object you are attempting to record in Super Slow-Mo) since this might trigger Super Slow-Mo recording in Auto mode. If there are moving objects in the on-screen square, you will not be able to record in Super Slow-mo.
- If you are filming in the fluorescent or flickering light, you should avoid doing so since it can cause the camera to record in super slow motion automatically. In addition to that, it can cause streaks or lines that flash when the video is played again.

- Make sure you record in an area that has enough light. We advise recording either in direct sunshine or under LED lights. While filming in a dark environment, the noise will be produced, and the camera can go into super slow-Mo mode by accident.

CHAPTER 10
HOW TO USE HYPERLAPSE/TIMELAPSE

What is Time-lapse?

The goal of a time-lapse movie is to condense the progression of motion over an extremely extended period into a relatively brief clip. Using a slow frame rate allows for this goal to be met. The standard frame rate for a motion picture is 24 frames per second, which means that the camera is effectively shooting 24 photographs every single second.

If you took 24 pictures per second of anything that moved more slowly, like a plant growing, you wouldn't see any movement at all. Now, let's imagine that you take a picture every hour and then piece them together. Your "24 frames per second" are now displaying the equivalent of 24 hours of growth in only one second.

When we speak about "**time-lapse**" on smartphones, we are often referring to "**hyper lapse**," which is a more accurate term. While creating a time-lapse, the camera is kept in a fixed location during the whole recording, and it does not move at any point. Since a hyper lapse is a time-lapse with the camera moving, the technique lends itself particularly well to use on mobile devices like smartphones.

Hyperlapse vs. Timelapse Photography: What's the Difference?

While they seem to serve the same function, you should not confuse the two. All timelapses compress time, but hyperlapses add a movement component.

The Basic Timelapse

The concept of a timelapse can be broken down into its parts quite simply. A video with a very slow frame rate can be seen here. When you watch a movie, you are treated to the visual equivalent of 24 still images every single second. Every frame will be represented by one twenty-fourth of a second. While not as rapid as the actual world, this is nevertheless quick enough for our brains to register a sense of fluid motion. As additional frames are added for each second, the motion gets smoother, and eventually, the picture resembles gazing through a window in an eerie way. This effect can be achieved by adding more frames.

This is good for things that happen on human time scales, but how would one go about capturing something like a plant emerging from the ground over some time? Since a plant doesn't grow much in a quarter of a second, you can snap a picture of it once a day for a year and then play back the pictures at a rate of 24 frames per second. A video of a plant that depicts a year's worth of development in just over 15 seconds would be produced if your camera remained in the same location during the whole recording, which is the assumption made here. There are a variety of aesthetic and scientific applications for time lapse photography, and nature documentaries are a terrific place to see it put to use. But, they do have certain restrictions when you wish to condense time from the perspective of a topic that is always moving.

Timelapse + Movement = Hyperlapse

You may have seen films in which a drone is flown over a crowded metropolis, and automobiles and people can be seen passing quickly below when the flight time is sped up to 30 seconds from the original 15-minute duration. The following is an example of a hyperlapse. A time lapse is everything that a hyperlapse is; the only difference is that the camera goes quite a distance in either direction.

While it may seem easy, there are numerous hurdles involved in making a hyperlapse appear decent. When you capture a time lapse, the camera remains completely still and steady during the whole process. If, on the other hand, you move about while holding the camera, the finished output will have a wobbly and disorganized aspect to it.

You will need to make use of specialized software to stabilize the final movie if you plan on creating a hyperlapse manually but by shooting individual photographs. Built-in stabilization is often found in cameras and drones that can automatically create hyperlapses for the user, such as those in the GoPro family of action cameras.

Another characteristic that distinguishes hyperlapses from traditional time-lapses is that the intervals that pass between photos are not always uniform. If you were producing a hyperlapse of a vacation, for instance, you would want to make the lengthy and uninteresting sections of the journey rush past, but you would want to slow things down somewhat if anything interesting was occurring.

Choosing the Right 'Lapse

It is not difficult to choose the appropriate timelapse style for your video. The thing you're capturing and the way you want the camera to travel are the two most important considerations here.

If the subject is going to remain in the frame for the whole of the shot and there is only one viewpoint that you need to capture, then you should utilize a standard timelapse. You can utilize a motion control rig to follow the subject's movement or present a new viewpoint of it if it is going to remain in one place or move extremely slowly. This option is useful in any case.

How to make a Timelapse on the Galaxy S23

Let's get started. To begin, launch the camera app on your Samsung Galaxy phone and choose "More" from the toolbar located at the bottom of the screen. The many modes of the camera are shown below for your convenience. "Hyperlapse" is one that we need.

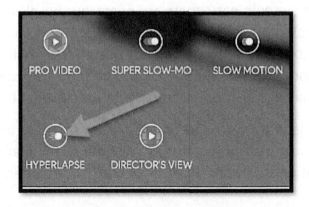

The recording process for a hyperlapse is the same as the recording process for any other video. To get started, press the shutter button.

A bright red bar will appear at the very top of the viewfinder while you are recording anything. This compares the amount of time that the camera has been rolling (the correct number) to the amount of time that the final hyperlapse will be (the left number).

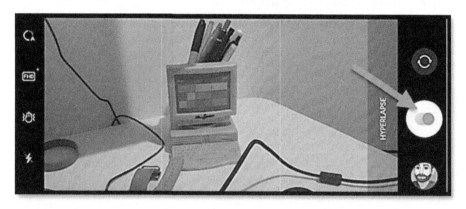

Adjust Hyperlapse speed

- From the home screen, choose Apps or swipe up to access your apps
- Choose Camera
- Choose MODE or swipe across the screen to select Hyperlapse mode.
- Tap the Hyperlapse speed icon.
- Choose the desired speed
- Tap the record button
- Tap the stop icon
- To view the captured Hyperlapse, choose the preview thumbnail

Activate or Deactivate a Timer

- From the home screen, choose Apps or swipe up to access your apps
- Choose Camera
- Choose Hyperlapse

- Choose MODE or swipe across the screen to select Hyperlapse mode.
- Tap the settings cog or the arrow icon
- Tap the timer icon
- Choose how long you'd like your timer to be set for
- Tap the back icon
- Tap the back icon again
- Your chosen timer will be displayed on the screen

CHAPTER 11

USING THE GALLERY APP ON A SMARTPHONE OR TABLET

How to look at pictures

If you spend an hour attempting to shoot the best possible selfie, you'll be able to examine the results of your labour in the Gallery and appreciate all of your hard work.

1. First, go to the Gallery and open it. Then, choose the **Pictures** option from the menu. Just on the image or video's thumbnail to open it in full-screen mode.
2. To look for a particular photo, hit the magnifying glass icon that's located in the top right corner of the screen. You can look for an image by using its tag, the name of its album, or any number of additional data.
3. A feature that allows photographs that have a similar appearance to be grouped is available. If this occurs, not all of your photographs will be shown on the Image tab; instead, you will see a little number in the corner of certain image thumbnails. This number might be 2, 3, or any other number. Just the thumbnail will bring up the collection of pictures that have been put together.
4. If you do not want to utilize this function and instead want all of your photographs to be shown, just press the symbol at the top of the screen that looks like a group of images that are similar to one another (it looks like a square).

Viewing and editing photos and videos

It is not necessary to have a degree in graphic design to improve your photographs.

You can make changes to them directly on your phone.

1. From the Gallery, choose the picture or video that you wish to modify by tapping its thumbnail.
2. Choose **Edit** (the symbol that looks like a pencil), and then alter the photo using the various tools that are offered.
3. Tap the icon labelled "**Undo**" or "**Redo**" to undo or redo the most recent modification. To reverse all of your adjustments, tap the Revert button.
4. To save your changes, press the Save button.

Move photos and videos to albums

Got a private interest that you're constantly keeping track of in a journal? **Place all of those photographs in a single location so that you can go back to them at a later time.**

1. From the **Gallery**, pick a picture by touching and holding it, and then tap **More** at the bottom of the screen.
2. After that, choose the photographs that you want to transfer and then press the Copy to album button. Instead, you can use the **Move to album** option to copy and paste the photographs into a separate album.
3. After that, choose the album that will contain the picture once it has been moved or pasted.
4. To make a new album, first, choose **Albums** from the bottom menu, and then select **"More options"** from the menu that appears (the three vertical dots). Tap **Create album**.

5. After giving the album a title, use the **Create** button to finish creating the album.

Delete photos and videos

You can get rid of the videos you don't need any more on your device to save up space. Here's how:

1. Launch the **Gallery app**.
2. Navigate to the photo or video you want to remove from your device.
3. Click the options button, and then select **Delete**.
4. Make the necessary confirmation and then the file would be gone.

Create an album

Your Gallery is starting to seem a bit jumbled since there are so many photographs in it. **Simply make an album to organize everything and get rid of the clutter.**

1. From the Gallery app, choose Albums; then, from the menu that appears, select **"More options"** (the three vertical dots); finally, select **Create album**.
2. Give your new album the title you want it to have, and then choose the Create button.
3. Touch the album itself when you want to add photos to your new album. Touch the **Add items** button, and then tap the Photos option in the resulting menu.
4. Choose the photographs you wish to upload, and then hit the **Done** button when you're finished.

Group albums

1. From the Gallery app, choose the **Albums** tab, and then at the top of the screen, press the **plus symbol** to add an album.
2. Tap **Group**. Tap the **Create** button once you have entered the appropriate name for your new group.

3. To add albums to your new group, touch the group, and then tap the **Add albums** button that appears underneath the group's name.
4. After that, choose the albums you want to listen to. When you are done, tap the **Add** button.

Use a Gallery widget

1) Go to the Home screen once you have downloaded the Gallery Widget from the Galaxy Store.
2) To access the settings for the Home screen, either taps and holds on the Home screen or swipe with your fingers to zoom out. Next, pick the **Widget** icon located at the bottom of the screen.
3) From the list of widgets, look for the word "**Gallery**." On the screen that displays the search results, press and holds the symbol that looks like a gallery, and then drag it to the Home screen.
4) Pick the photographs that will be shown on the Gallery Widget and make any necessary adjustments to their sizes.

Gallery settings

1) To access the home screen on your Android mobile phone, you must first press the "**Home**" button.
2) Choose "**Menu**" from the drop-down menu, and then select the "**Gallery**" icon. There will be a list of all of the albums that are currently saved on your phone.
3) To bring up a menu at the bottom of the screen, you must first press the "**Menu**" button. Put your finger on the album that has the parameters you want to modify.
4) To see the various configuration options, tap the "**Menu**" button, then touch the "**More**" button. Inside the album's settings, there is the option to use a photo as a contact or as the background on your device.
5) To preserve your modified configuration, tap the "**Save**" button.

Create Stories

- Hit **"Stories"** in the Gallery app.
- Select **More options** from the menu (three vertical dots).
- Select **"Settings"** from the menu.
- Toggle the **"Auto-generate stories"** switch on.
- Allow your Galaxy smartphone to generate stories based on your images and videos by enabling this feature.

Users can also make their own stories by selecting their images and videos:

To see the options, repeat the procedures outlined above.

- Tap **"Create a narrative,"** give it a title, and then choose the photographs you want to include in it.

Share photos and videos

Quick Share is a feature on your device that allows you to share items between your device and other devices.

Here's how to make use of it:

1. Go to the other device you want to send the video or photo to and then open the Quick Settings panel.
2. Navigate to the **Quick Share** icon and click on it.
3. **Enable the feature by selecting from any of the following options:**

- **Contacts only**: Use this option if the transfer is between two people with each other's numbers on their contacts list.
- **Anyone nearby**: Use this option if the number of the person you're sharing the item with is not registered on your device.

4. Go to your device, and navigate to the photo or image you'd like to share in your Gallery app.
5. Click the share icon and then select the option that's "**Quick Share**."
6. Wait until the name of the person shows up, and then click on it.
7. Go over to the other phone and click **Accept**.

CHAPTER 12
USES OF AR ZONE IN S23

The S23 Series and the majority of Samsung smartphones now offer the amazing picture feature known as AR Zone.

In addition to other AR-related features, AR Zone contains an AR Emoji Camera, AR Doodle, AR Emoji Studio, AR Emoji Stickers, Deco Photo, and more. Nevertheless, certain features are only available dependent on the service provider or model. You can now use AR emojis as profile pictures in Samsung accounts and contacts thanks to Samsung AR Zone. You can choose from more than 10 places, create your feelings, and make use of the many category themes.

- Switch on your Samsung camera.
- Go to **More** with a Swipe
- **Go to AR Zone and tap it. There are the following functionalities available:**

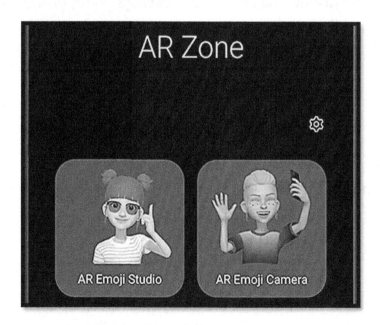

➢ **AR Emoji Camera:** Create your My Emoji avatar using the camera.

- **AR Doodle:** Add line drawings or handwriting to your surroundings to enhance films. AR Doodle follows you around by tracking your face and space.
- **AR Emoji Studio:** Create and personalize your My Emoji avatar with augmented reality tools.
- **AR Emoji Stickers:** Customize your My Emoji avatar with AR stickers.
- **Deco Pic:** Use the camera to decorate photographs or movies in real-time.

AR Emoji Camera:

- Open your phone's camera and go to the **AR Zone**.
- Select **AR Emoji Camera** from the menu.
- Choose the emoji you want to use and the mode you want to use.
- **Depending on the emoji you choose, the available options may change.**
    - **SCENE:** An emoji imitates your facial emotions. You can also alter the appearance of the backdrop.
    - **MASK:** The emoji's face overlays yours, giving the impression that you're wearing a mask.
    - **MIRROR:** The emoji imitates your actions.
    - **PLAY:** The emoji moves against a real-world backdrop.
- To take a photo, tap and hold the emoji symbol, or to record a video, tap and hold the icon.
- In the Gallery, you can see and share the photos and movies you've taken.

AR Doodle:

- Go to **Samsung Camera's AR Zone**.
- Press the **AR Doodle** button.
- The recognition area appears on the screen when the camera identifies the person.
- To write or draw in the recognition area, tap the **drawing icon**.
- You can also write or draw outside the recognition area if you switch to the back camera.
- You can record yourself doodling if you press the record button and then start scribbling.

- To record a video, use the **record** button.
- To stop recording the video, use the **stop** button.
- You can watch and share the video.

AR Emoji Studio:

- Go to the AR Zone and click on it.
- Open the **AR Emoji Studio app**.
    - You can choose from a variety of pre-made emojis to get started immediately.
- Swipe left or right to choose an emoji, then press the arrow that appears.
- Take a **selfie** or choose an image if you want to create your emoji.
- To make an emoji, follow the on-screen directions.

Make a short AR emoji video and use it to adorn your device:

- Turn on the **Samsung camera's** AR Zone.
- Open the **AR Emoji Studio app**.
- Select **Make a movie**, a **lock screen**, or **a call screen**.
- Choose a template that you wish to use.
- Tap the **Gallery button** to change the background picture.
- To save the video, tap **Save. (NB: In the Gallery, you can see the videos you've saved)**.
- Select an option at the bottom of the screen to use the video immediately.

Create a contact profile with an AR emoji:

- Open the **Camera app** and go to the AR Zone.
- Launch the **AR Emoji Studio app**.
- Go to **Profile** and choose an emoji.
- Capture your emotion or choose the desired posture.
- Save by tapping **Done**.

AR Emoji Sticker:

- Open the camera app on your phone and choose **AR Zone**.
- Select **AR Emoji Stickers** from the menu.
- At the top of the sticker list, tap **(+)**.

- Make any changes you wish to the stickers and then save them.
- By tapping **Custom**, you can see the stickers you've made.

Delete AR emoji stickers:

- Go to Samsung Camera's AR Zone.
- Select **AR Emoji Stickers** from the menu.
- Select **Delete Stickers** from the three-dot menu.
- Tap Delete after selecting the emoji stickers you want to remove.

Using AR emoji stickers in chats:

- Tap the Samsung keyboard when writing a message in the Messages app.
- Press and hold the emoji symbol.
- Choose an emoji sticker from your collection.
- The emoji sticker will be placed on the card.

Deco Image:

- Turn on the Samsung camera's AR Zone.
- Select Deco Pic from the menu. The following is a list of resources:
  - GIFs
  - Masks
  - Frames
  - Stamps

Using Director's View

Director's View allows you to choose your angles and control your shots like a pro. By switching cameras, you can record videos from different perspectives.

While shooting a movie, you can examine each camera's scenes via thumbnails and adjust them by pressing the thumbnails.

Multi-camera standby

You can capture more of your scene and create a more compelling narrative with the new video tools. Similar to a talented movie director, you can switch between different viewpoints while you're making a film and use both the front-facing and rear-facing cameras simultaneously. You can record yourself while shooting others while making a group video for a certain occasion, such as a birthday party or a historical site. From a variety of recording perspectives, including Ultra Wide, Wide, and Tele, you can view live thumbnails. Just touch the thumbnails to move between cameras.

Vlogger mode

Dual recording with front and back cameras gives you additional alternatives, particularly for Vloggers, since Director's View enables you to record from several camera lenses at the same time. Dual-recorded vlogs may make your content more engaging and interactive.

Director's View: How to Shoot

Step 1: Go to the camera.
Step 2: Select MORE > **DIRECTOR'S VIEW** from the list of shooting modes.
Step 3: Select the desired camera thumbnail.
Step 4:. To change the screen mode, hit the Change screen mode icon in the top right corner and choose one of three options: PIP (Picture-in-picture), Split view, or Single view.
Step 5: To record a video, press the **Record** button. By touching the thumbnail, you can change the camera while recording. Tap the Display button to see the thumbnail if it is hidden.

Step 6: To stop recording the video, press the Stop button.

CHAPTER 13
EDIT PHOTOS AND VIDEOS

Face effects

You should bear in mind that you can only access this option when there is a face on the screen, especially for selfies pictures.

1. Launch the **Gallery** app on your device and get to the photo with the face you'd like to customize.
2. Click the icon at the top section of the screen that says "**Edit**," select more options from the list provided, and then click on the option, "**Face effects**."
3. From the list provided, you will be able to select different editing options for your face, such as **Smoothness, Tone, and Fix red-eyes**.
4. Select any one of the options displayed, and then adjust the slider to how much you want the effect to be applied to your photo.
5. Click the **Done** button after making your edits.
6. If you're not okay with what you've made, you can click the **Revert** button to start all over or end it.
7. Click **Save** when you're satisfied.

Object eraser

This editing option can be used to take off the items you don't want to be seen in the background of your photo.

1. Launch the Gallery app on your device and get to the photo you'd like to apply edits to.
2. Click on the icon that says "**Edit**," select more options from the list displayed, and then select the option, "**Object eraser**."
3. Now, draw a line around the item you'd like to remove from the photo, and then click on the Erase button.
4. If you make any mistakes, you can click on the undo and redo arrows at the top of the screen. Take off all the items you don't need in the photo and then click **Done** when you're done.

5. If you're not okay with what you've made or you want to start from the beginning, you can click the **Revert** button to go back to the original state of the photo.
6. When you're satisfied with what you have done, click the **Save** button.

Spot colour

With this editing option, you will be able to add or remove the colours you need or don't need from your photos.

Here's how to go about it:

1. Launch the Gallery app on your device and get to the photo you'd like to apply this edit to.
2. Click the icon at the top of the screen that says "**Edit**," select **More options**, and then click on the option, "**Spot colour**." After clicking on the option, all the colours on the photo will turn black and white; click on the area you'd like to apply the colour edit.
3. If you want to remove the original colour on that area from the photo, click the option that says "**Remove colour**" and if you want to add colour to that area, click the option that says "**Add colour**."
4. If you want to do this manually, you can click on the Eraser icon at the top of the screen, adjust the slider to your preferred size, and then rub it against the area you want to apply edits to.

5. Click **Done** when you're finished.
6. If you're not okay with what you have or you want to start from the beginning, you can click on the Revert button to take you back to the original photo.
7. Once you're okay with the edits, click **Save**.

Style

You can also add some filter effects to your photos right on your device, using the Style option:

1. Open up the Gallery app on your device and get to the photo you'd like to apply the edits to.
2. Click the icon at the top that says "**Edit**," select **More options**, and then click on the option that says "**Style**."
3. Swipe until you get to the filter you'd like to use on the photo and then click on it.
   Note: You can click Original to compare it with the previous photo; this way you'll be able to get the differences.
4. After picking a filter, the next thing to do is to select the extent you'd like for it to be applied to the photo.
5. You can click on the paintbrush icon if you'd like to draw on the photo and if you want to take off the drawing from the photo, click the **eraser icon.**
6. You can use the icons, Background only, and Subject only to compare what you have with the previous version of the images.
7. Click **done** when you've finished.
8. If you're not okay with what you have and want to start all over, you can click on the **Revert** button to go back to the original picture.
9. Click **Save** when you're done with the editing.

Colour mix

If you don't like the way the colours are in your photo, you can use the Colour Mix option to blend and adjust their intensity.

1. Launch the Gallery app and get to the photo you'd like to apply the edits to.

2. Click on the icon at the top that says "**Edit**," select **More options**, and click on **Colour mix**.
3. Click on the colour you'd like to apply the edits to at the bottom, and then move the slider based on how much you want the intensity to be.

4. Select the options, **Hue, Saturation, or Luminance**, and apply the effects as much as you need on the photo.
5. You can apply this colour mix setting to as many colours as you want on the photo.
6. Click **Done** once you're done.
7. If you're not okay with what you have and want to go back to the beginning, you can click on the **Revert** button.
8. Click **Save** once you're done.

Video Editing

The video editor on your device provides you with several options to customize and enhance your videos.

1. Open Video Editor

Launch the Gallery app on your device and get to the video you'd like to apply the edits to, and then click on the **Pencil icon** and you will be taken to the Video Editor menu. From here, you will be able to access different editing options for the video.

2. Trim the length of a video

From the first screen that shows up after you open the video editor, you will be able to shorten the length of the video you selected. First, click on the **Scissors icon** displayed at the top, and then adjust the white bars at the bottom of the screen to edit the length of the video.

3. Edit video speed

You can also adjust the speed of videos on your device by speeding it up or slowing it down. Click on the scissor icon displayed at the bottom section of the screen, and then select from the different speeds displayed at the top i.e. 1x, 2x, and 1/2x.

4. Crop video

In the same way, you crop photos and images; you can also crop videos on your device to get rid of those unnecessary parts by the side. All you have to do is click on the Transform tool, and then adjust the border to the size you want.

5. Rotate video

While you're still on the Transform tool page, click on the **rotate** icon displayed next to the crop icon to rotate the video.

6. Flip video

The Flip tool is the third option displayed beside the Crop and Rotate tools. With this option, you will be able to flip the video in any direction of your choice.

7. Adjust aspect ratio

You can also make changes to the aspect ratio of the videos on your device. With this tool, you will be able to crop your videos in the dimension of your choice.

Launch the **Transform tool** and then click on the icon with the options listed Free, 1:1, 4:9, and so on; this is where you can select the aspect ratio dimension of your choice.

8. Add filters

Pictures are not the only files you can add filters to, you can also add filters to your videos. Open up the video editor menu and click on the filter icon to select any filter of your choice.

9. Blur video

You can also blur a section or part of your video using the video editor on your device.

- Navigate to the **Emoji tool** and then click on the **Mosaic pen** icon.
- You will be presented with a bar at the bottom of the screen; click on the **Blur pen** to select, and then draw on the area on the video you want to be blurred.

10. Save video

When you're done with all the edits you want to apply to your video, click on the option by the top left section of the screen, "**Save as copy**" to save the video to your device.

Additional tools for editing photos/videos

1. Adobe Premiere Rush

Users can produce films on the move that is of professional quality using the sophisticated Adobe Premiere Rush app, which is a video editing program. You can also use it to create transitions to movies, apply filters and effects, edit, chop, and combine video clips, and more. It includes capabilities for colour correction, audio editing, and motion graphics editing among its extensive collection of editing tools.

This program has some useful features, one of which is the capability to synchronize projects across all platforms. This makes it simple to transition between editing on a mobile device and a desktop computer.

2. Kinemaster

Kinemaster is a well-known video editing application that provides users with a variety of editing capabilities, such as multi-track audio, 3D transitions, and voiceovers, which make it simple to produce films that are of professional quality. You can use it to add text, photos, and music to your videos, in addition to applying a variety of filters and effects. You can also use it to edit your videos. The ability to add numerous layers of video, photos, and stickers to the finished film to make it more dynamic is the app's defining characteristic. In addition to that, it is capable of capturing video and audio in real-time and it supports the 4K video resolution.

3. PowerDirector

PowerDirector is a feature-rich video editing application that provides powerful editing features, such as motion tracking, colour correction, and keyframe animation. These tools enable you to transform your raw material into films that look fantastic. Moreover, it enables the creation of 360-degree videos and comes with a comprehensive collection of special effects and transitions. This software offers some useful features, one of which is the capability to generate individualized titles and visuals. In addition, the application has multi-track editing, Chroma keying, and a video stabilizer that is integrated right in.

4. LumaFusion

LumaFusion is a robust and professional mobile video editing tool that is now officially accessible for Android smartphones. It was previously only available for iOS. It provides a full collection of features for generating and editing high-quality videos, such as multi-track editing (layer up to 6 video and 6 audio tracks), colour correction, audio mixing, titling tools, and the capability to use multiple touch screens, to name just a few of these features.

Also, the software is compatible with external storage devices and provides users the ability to directly export content to well-known social networking networks. In addition to that, it has a Storyblocks Library that has hundreds of pieces of royalty-free music, sound effects, films, and backdrops, as well as a media library that contains full information.

LumaFusion is a sophisticated and adaptable tool that can be used by anybody wishing to edit movies on the move, including content makers, journalists, and anyone else.

5. Filmora

Filmora is a program for editing films that is simple to use and provides a variety of tools for producing videos of professional quality. These capabilities include colour grading, motion tracking, and audio editing, among others. You can also use it to add text, graphics, and music to your videos, as well as edit, chop, and combine video clips. In addition to that, you can choose from a wide range of filters and overlays. It provides capabilities such as the capability to add dynamic text and images to movies, making the films more interesting to watch. In addition to that, it has a broad variety of special effects to choose from and allows editing of 4K videos.

6. Inshot

InShot is a well-known video editing application that provides its users with a variety of editing options, including video trimming, cropping, filters, and music, in addition to the capacity to add text and emojis to their creations. In addition to this, it enables users to modify the video speed and add slow-motion effects, as well as provide them with a selection of visual effects such as glitch, retro, and neon. In addition to that, it allows you to change the speed of the movie and rotate it. The capability of the InShot app to modify the video aspect ratio so that it is compatible with other social media networks, such as Instagram, TikTok, and YouTube, is one of the program's standout features.

7. Quik

Quik is a video editing tool that was created by GoPro. Using Quik, you can quickly and simply make films using the footage captured by your GoPro camera. It comes with a selection of different themes and layouts for you to pick from.

The capacity of the software to automatically analyse the footage and produce a film with matching music and effects is one of the app's distinctive features. This makes it simple for users to create videos that seem to have been created by professionals in a short amount of time.

In addition to that, it gives users the ability to change the pace at which the video plays and provides a selection of different video formats.

8. VivaCut

VivaCut is a professional video editing program that provides a variety of complex editing capabilities, such as chroma keying, masking, and keyframe animations. Because of this, it is a favourite option among content producers for social media platforms and filmmakers. Moreover, the software gives users the option to construct video collages, which consist of many films being played concurrently on the display screen.

The capability of the VivaCut app to alter the video aspect ratio so that it is compatible with various social media sites, such as Instagram, TikTok, and YouTube, is one of the app's standout features.

9. Splice

Splice is an impressive video editor that makes it simple for users to produce visually attractive videos. It provides tools for editing, chopping, and combining video, as well as tools for altering the pace of playback, as well as tools for adding music, text, titles, and voiceovers to videos.

The software has been streamlined for use on mobile devices and offers editing capabilities comparable to that of a desktop pro. Users can input photographs and videos, arrange and mix them using a user-friendly timeline, and then generate high-quality films from the application.

Splice allows users to modify the aspect ratio of their videos so that they are compatible with a variety of social media networks, including Instagram, TikTok, and Snapchat, which is a really handy tool. It also supports 4K video editing and has an easy-to-use interface, making it simple for novices to make films that are of professional quality.

10. Magisto

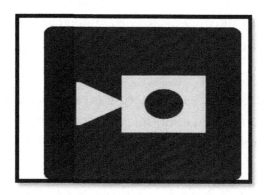

Magisto is a cutting-edge tool for editing films that makes use of artificial intelligence to automatically edit and generate movies of a professional standard.

In addition to the ability to add captions and logos, it provides a variety of editing tools, such as video cutting, filters, and music, as well as other options. The app features a function for editing that is driven by AI. This feature examines the footage and then automatically builds a movie complete with music, effects, and transitions. This feature makes it simple for users to create films that look beautiful in a short amount of time. Customers have access to a variety of video types and the ability to tailor the playback of the video to their tastes.

11. Shotcut

ShotCut is a powerful video editor and creator that gives users the ability to generate hip music videos with special effects and animations that can be shared on social media sites such as Instagram, YouTube, and others.

The application provides standard editing capabilities such as trimming, cutting, and combining in addition to sophisticated features like chroma keying, keyframing, Picture-in-Picture (PIP), and other similar functions.

The user can produce visually beautiful films, add text and animated text, and quickly post their works on social media sites without the inclusion of watermarks.

The user has access to more than 250 video effects and vintage filters.

Set a photo or video as wallpaper

How to Set a Video as Your Lock Screen Wallpaper

To set a video as the background of your Lock screen, you do not need the assistance of any other program. You can do so right from inside the app that Samsung calls the Gallery.

Here's what you need to do:

1. Launch the **Samsung Gallery app**, and choose the video that you would want to watch.

2. Choose "**Set as wallpaper**" followed by "**Lock screen**" from the menu accessible by tapping the three dots.
3. If your video is too lengthy, hit the symbol that looks like scissors to cut it down to less than 15 seconds, and then touch the **Done** button once you're through. It is important to keep in mind that the size of live video wallpaper cannot exceed 100 MB.
4. After you are finished, touch the Set on Lock screen option, and then you are ready to go.

Set a Video as Your Home Screen Wallpaper

Setting a video as your Home screen wallpaper is slightly more complicated than doing so for the Lock screen. To do so, you will need to download an additional app.

You can use Samsung Good Lock, which is an all-in-one customizing app developed by Samsung. You will not find it pre-installed on Samsung smartphones; however, it is available for purchase through the Galaxy Store.

After it's downloaded, go with the instructions that are listed below.

It is important to keep in mind that this method is a bit of a workaround since the program does not directly let putting movies as your home screen background.

1. Open up **Good Lock** and go to the **Family** menu to locate the **Wonderland** module. When you touch the module, the application will take you to the Galaxy Store so that you can download and install the module.
2. Launch **Wonderland**, then go to the "**New**" menu and pick "**Gallery**." Don't worry, the picture you choose won't show up in the final product
3. Choose **Video** by tapping the **App to Layer** icon located in the lower right-hand corner of your screen. Choose the movie you want from your collection, make any necessary adjustments to its duration, and then touch the **Done** button. The movie will show up on top of the picture that you selected earlier in the process. Then, resize the video so that it fills the screen preview, and then

hit the **Save** button. Just give this user-defined pre-set a name, and then hit Save once again.
4. After everything is finished, you will then be shown a sample of your video wallpaper. Once you are pleased with the outcome, hit the **Set as wallpaper** button, and then choose whether you want to apply it to only the home screen or both the home screen and the lock screen.
5. If you're not satisfied with the result, you can always return to the **Wonderland module** and make changes to the pre-set you've already stored there.

Before you use a movie as your wallpaper, check that it has a high enough quality and is the right size. If it does not, the result can be a pixelated or otherwise unclear image. For instance, if your smartphone has a screen with a resolution of QHD and you utilize a movie with a quality of Full HD, the wallpaper may not seem very well.

CHAPTER 14
RECORD, EDIT, AND SHARE 8K VIDEO ON GALAXY PHONE

8K Video Recording and Editing

8K video is the most recent and highest-quality image standard that is currently available, and devices like the Galaxy S23 and Note20 5G are capable of recording films in this remarkable format. You are also able to edit your movies in any way that you see fit, all while keeping the quality high and eliminating any blur.

You'll have access to extra editing options, and on some of the compatible devices, you'll even be able to choose which microphone is being used to record. You can upload your new films to YouTube or your smart television if you want to show them off to the rest of the world.

Note that transferring 8K video from a computer to a TV via an HDMI USB-C connection is not supported. While shooting videos in 4K or 8K resolution, the only place they can be kept is on the phone's internal memory.

You will need to activate the 8K option in the Camera app on your device before you can record a video in 8K resolution on it. After that, you can cut and edit your video using the Editor. In addition to that, the Pro Video capability can also be used to take still images at an 8K resolution.

As a result of enhancements made to its low light capture as well as its 3X optical zoom magnification, the Galaxy S23 series is capable of producing the most crystal clear 8K films to date.

1. To start taking a video, open the **Camera** app.
2. Go to the VIDEO menu, and then choose the Resolution icon to change the resolution to 8K.

3. When you are ready, hit the **Record** button to start the recording.
4. If you want to save a high-resolution snapshot while you're shooting an 8K movie, you can do so by tapping the **Capture** button.
5. After you have completed recording, you should open the Gallery app and look for the video you just recorded.
6. When the video is playing, touch the screen many times after clicking the **Play** button on the video.
7. To snap high-resolution 33MP photographs of the movie, tap the **Gallery** button located in the upper left corner of the screen.

Take note that you can use the Gallery app at a later time to examine the picture's resolution. Just find the photo you want to see, and then swipe upward.

The recommended resolution is 4320 x 7680 pixels.

8. To make changes to the video, hit the **Edit** button (the pencil icon).
9. Next, trim your movie using the slider located at the bottom of the screen. Touch the speaker icon to change the volume of the sound or add some music as the backdrop.
10. If you do not want the movie to be shown at 8K quality, you can change the resolution to anything else. Select the **More options**

button (it looks like three vertical dots), then hit **Size and format**, and finally select the resolution you want to use.
11. After you are through making changes, press the **Save** button. Depending on how large the movie is, saving it might take a few minutes of your time.
12. After recording an 8K video or picture, use the Gallery app to see the specific resolution characteristics of the media. Select the movie or picture that you want to see, and then swipe up on it to access its information.

While recording videos, you not only have control over the sound input, but you can also modify the direction that the microphone is facing.

Share 8K video

Remember that to share the movie, both your phone and your TV need to have their Wi-Fi switched on. It is time to publish your video so that everyone can see it and appreciate it. You can either do this wirelessly on your **Smart TV** or upload it to YouTube. Both options are available to you.

You can use either Tap view or Smart View to transmit the video you are watching to your television. With **Tap view**, you can rapidly transfer media from your phone to your TV by tapping your phone near the edge of your Screen. Instead, you can activate **Smart View** to reflect the display of your phone on your television.

Rather than hosting it on your website, you can consider uploading it to YouTube. Launch the Gallery app first, and then choose your video from the menu that appears. To access the YouTube app, hit the Share button at the bottom of the screen, and then tap the YouTube icon. After logging into your account, all you need to do is follow the on-screen instructions to submit your movie. Because of the size of the file, uploading the movie can take some time.

CHAPTER 15
CUSTOMIZE THEMES AND ICONS

Download theme

1. Tap and hold a space on your **Home** screen to access the Home screen settings menu.
2. Tap **Themes**.
3. Tap icons and browse for the icon pack you'd like to use.
4. Tap **Download**.
5. Tap **Apply**.

Change theme

You've been developing that idea for a considerable amount of time.

If you already have another theme downloaded or stored, all you need to do to change your theme is, apply the one you have downloaded or saved.

- Touch and hold an empty place on the Home screen, and then choose **Themes** from the menu that appears. Tap the **Menu** icon (it looks like three horizontal lines), then press **my stuff**, and then tap **Themes** to see all of the themes you have available to you.
- Choose the theme you want to use, go over the details, and then hit the **Apply** button. Tap the Apply button once again, if necessary, to confirm your selection.

Please take note that once you have applied a theme, it cannot be removed. If you do not want to continue using it, you will need to either use the default theme or switch to a different theme.

Download icon

Want to show off your passion for your favourite hobby? Try customizing your phone by downloading new icons.

Touch and hold an empty place on the **Home** screen, and then choose **Themes** from the menu that appears. Touch the **Icons** button, slide up to see all of the available icons, and then choose the icon that you want to download.

Touch the **Download** button if the icon set is available for free, or hit the price (such as **$0.99**) if it must be purchased. You can either **select a Payment Method** or **Use discounts**. If this is the first time you've used Themes, read the information that's been provided, and then hit the Proceed button. To confirm, tap the **Pay now** button.

Change icon

Maybe you've grown a bit weary of looking at those symbols. If you already have another set of icons downloaded or stored, all you need to do to apply it is follow these instructions. If you wish to replace your icons.

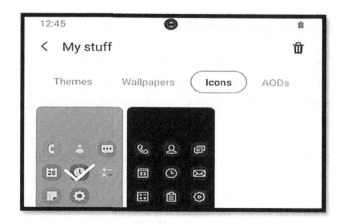

To access a space, tap and hold a spot on the Home screen. Then, choose **Themes**, and then select **Icons**. Tap the Menu symbol (it looks like three horizontal lines), then press **My Stuff**, and then hit Icons under **My stuff**. This will bring you a list of all of your icons. Choose the icons you want to use, and then choose the **Apply** button.

Remove theme

Sorry, it seems like you accidentally downloaded the incorrect theme. Just erase it; there is no need to keep a record of it.

Touch and hold an empty place on the Home screen, and then choose Themes from the menu that appears. First, choose the Menu icon (it looks like three horizontal lines), then select Bought products from the drop-down menu. Choose the theme or themes you want to get rid of, and then tap the Delete icon (it looks like a trash can) in the top right corner of the screen. To confirm, tap the Erase button at the bottom.

Delete icon

You are free to erase icons whenever you want if you change your mind. Just tap and hold an empty region of the screen when you're on a Home screen. After selecting Themes from the list, choose the **Menu** icon (the three horizontal lines). Choose **Purchased items**, and then select Icons from the drop-down menu. You can delete unwanted icons by tapping the **Delete icon** (it looks like a trash can) in the top right corner of the screen and then selecting those icons. To confirm, tap the **Erase button** at the bottom.

Restore purchased themes

Nobody wants to spend their money more than once on the same product. If you link your phone to your Samsung account, you will be able to retrieve any things that you have already bought, even if you did it on a different device.

Touch and hold an empty place on the Home screen, and then choose **Themes** from the menu that appears. First, choose the Menu icon (it looks like three horizontal lines), then select **Purchased items** from the drop-down menu. Click the **Download** button that is located next to the theme that you wish to restore on your phone. You are free to carry out the procedure as many times as necessary.

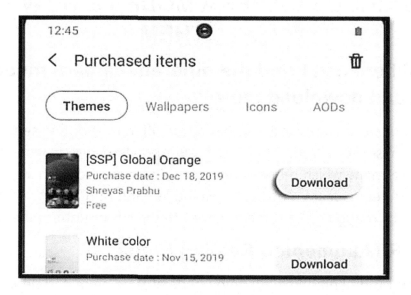

Note: You can recover purchased wallpapers or icons from the same page. Simply use the menu at the top of the screen.

CHAPTER 16
VARIOUS CAMERA MODES & HOW TO USE THEM

Where can I find the different camera modes and can I download more?

Your camera app probably has a few different shooting settings you can choose from. Your model and the operating system you're using will determine which modes are accessible to you. You can switch between different camera modes by swiping left and right on the camera screen or by dragging the camera modes to the left or right of the screen.

AR (Augmented Reality) Emoji

AR (Augmented Reality) Emoji generates an animated depiction of you that can then be used to capture your motions and facial expressions. Emoji AR was developed by Nintendo. You can locate the AR Emoji feature on your smartphone if it supports it by opening the camera app, then selecting AR Emoji from the menu that appears.

Fast Motion/Hyperlapse

A video can be recorded in rapid motion, and then it can be played back at a speed that is far quicker than the original.

- First, open the camera, and then choose **Fast motion** from the menu.
- Tap the record icon, to begin filming your fast-motion video
- When you have finished filming, tap the **stop icon**
- You'll need to press the quick view box to modify the portion of the video that you wish to play in fast forward. You can also access your video using the application titled Gallery.
- First, choose the video you want to edit, and then hit the **watch** button.

- Next, use the sliders at the bottom of the screen to pick the segment of the movie that you want to play again at a faster speed.
- Finally, when you're done, tap the **export or save** button.

Flaw detection

Flaw detection is an intelligent camera function that will warn you if it finds anything strange about a photo, allowing you to shoot the image again with the option to correct the flaw. If you are unable to use the fault detection tool on your device, you can replace it with the shot recommendations and scene optimizer options instead.

There are four types of flaw-detection notifications:

- **Eyeblink** measures the eye size in the preview. It then detects any change in eye size when the shutter clicks, to check if anyone is blinking
- **Motion Blur** detects any blur caused by moving subjects or shaky hands
- **Lens smudge** detects any dirt on the camera lens. This notice will only be displayed once within the first 10 seconds of opening the Camera app
- **Backlight** detects saturated areas of the image. For example, if there's a bright light in the background

Steps

- Open the camera, then tap the settings cog
- Tap the switch to enable or disable Flaw detection
- A notification will be displayed if an error has been detected

Please note: Blink and blur detection work best when there are up to three people in the frame and the subject is up to 1.5 meters away from the camera. The lens smudges and backlight detection notifications can only appear once within 24 hours.

Live Focus/Portrait Mode

You have direct control over the bokeh effect, which enables you to modify the degree of background blur in real-time thanks to live focus, which provides you direct control over the bokeh effect. It is also possible to make adjustments to the blur after the picture has been taken, ensuring that you will always receive the best possible photograph.

- First, launch your camera and pick Live Focus.
- Then, tap the effect you want to use.
- To snap a picture, press the shutter button on your camera, and then adjust the blur by sliding the slider to the left or right.

Please note that for the best results, the subject should be between one and one and a half meters away from the camera lens.

- To snap your picture, press the capture button. You can make adjustments to the blurriness of your Live focus images in the Gallery, if you are dissatisfied with the picture after it has been taken.

- Choose Gallery
- Select a picture captured with Live focus.
- Tap Change background effect.

Please take notice that this selection will only be available for images that were captured using the Live focus mode.

- You can make adjustments to your picture by choosing a new blur effect and sliding the slider to vary the amount of blur.
- After making your changes, you can save the image by clicking the **Apply** button.

Scene Optimizer

The scene optimizer is an intelligent photo assistant that can automatically recognize what is in the frame and modify the settings of your camera to help you take the best possible picture in the situation. The Scene Optimiser feature allows you to make changes to a variety of parameters while also choosing from over 30 different modes to find the option that works best with your picture.

Optimized scenes include Food, Animals, Sky, Watersides, Snow, Portraits, Landscapes, Mountains, Street scenes, Birds, and Flowers.

Greenery, Beaches, Night scenes, Backlit, Indoor scenes, Tress, Sunrises and sunsets, Waterfalls, Text, Clothing, Vehicle, Face, Drink, People, Cat, Shoe, Dog, Stage, and Baby.

- Launch your camera, and then hit the settings icon to access the options, and then select **Scene Optimiser**.
- Touch the switch to set the **Scene optimizer** on.
- After the Scene optimizer has been on, you can start the Document scan by pressing the switch. Please note: if the Scene optimizer option is unavailable, try switching to the rear-facing camera.
- If the **Scene optimizer** has been switched on in the settings, it can be instantly activated and disabled by touching the symbol at the bottom right of the screen. Document scan enables you to scan paper documents and save them as photos without any distortion. When the function is switched on and off, a notice will display to indicate the change.

Telephone Mode

Telephoto lenses, in contrast to cameras with digital zoom, enable you to zoom in on a scene or a single subject without losing any of the details in the image. This gives you the flexibility to come closer to your subject without worrying about how the image will turn out.

Because of the short depth of field that is produced by telephoto lenses, it is simple to blur the backdrop and put the focus on the subject of your photograph.

- To use the telephoto lens, tap its symbol. It will have the appearance of a leaf.
- To snap a picture, you need to click the **capture** button.

CHAPTER 17
USING SAMSUNG EXPERT RAW TO IMPROVE YOUR PHOTOGRAPHY

What is Samsung Expert RAW?

The advanced camera software for Samsung's Galaxy handsets is called Expert RAW. The software, which was made available on February 25, 2022, upgrades some of Samsung's most recent flagship devices with some additional photographic capabilities and settings.

Samsung Camera App vs. Expert RAW

What is Samsung Expert Raw?

Samsung's Galaxy devices are equipped with a sophisticated camera app called Expert RAW. The software was made available for download on February 25, 2022, and it adds a variety of additional photography-related capabilities and controls to chosen models of Samsung's most recent flagship smartphones.

Expert RAW is designed for more experienced photographers and is based on the RAW picture format. It has a broader dynamic range, which allows for more information to be captured in both bright and dark portions of a shot, as well as the most editing capabilities. In comparison, each of these 16-bit RAW picture files might be between 10MB and 30MB, whilst the JPEGs produced by the normal program produce less than 3MP. To get the most out of these photographs, you need to be comfortable with RAW editing tools such as Lightroom or Photoshop. This is because the greater file sizes are utilized for editing rather than sharing. As compared to the camera software that comes pre-installed on Samsung smartphones, the app includes manual camera features that allow users to put their unique imprint on the photos they take. Manual settings are provided by Samsung Expert RAW for ISO, shutter speed, EV, metering, and white balance. These options will assist you in achieving the ideal exposure, regardless of whether you are photographing static or action scenarios. Naturally, this is in addition to compatibility with the RAW file format. To put it another way, Expert RAW acts as a portal through which users can access a larger universe of more advanced photographic tools and adjustments.

How to get Samsung Expert RAW on your phone

Before you can download the Samsung Expert RAW software, you will need to fulfil a few requirements first. To get started, you'll need to have a Samsung Galaxy phone that's compatible with the software. The next step is to create a Samsung account on your device. As long as these two requirements are satisfied, you will not be charged to get Expert RAW from Samsung's Galaxy Store. You won't be able to purchase Expert RAW from Google Play or any other third-party retailer that operates similarly.

Expert RAW vs. a standard camera app

The two different camera applications, Expert RAW and Samsung's default camera app have an astonishing amount of features in common. Both are fully equipped with the manual camera settings that have been discussed before, such as ISO, EV, and shutter speed choices. You'll find both of these settings and the ability to manually peak the focus in the "**Pro**" mode of the app's default configuration.

You'll also notice that the zoom numbers at the bottom of the screen have been replaced with letter icons to represent each of the camera's four lenses. This is something you'll be able to see for yourself. **Pro and Expert RAW** do not try to choose the optimal lens setting for the current scene based on the lighting circumstances as the default mode of the regular app does. Instead, they lock you into the lens that you select. This additional control has both positive and negative effects on the image's clarity and exposure. The default camera software that comes pre-installed on Samsung devices also has an option for RAW format output. It is also crucial to note that Expert RAW does not have several features that are cornerstones of the experience of using a current mobile camera, such as a specialized mode for taking portraits, shooting at night, or even a video mode. The software does not allow you to take selfies or record videos of any kind. Thus, why bother downloading that extra application in the first place?

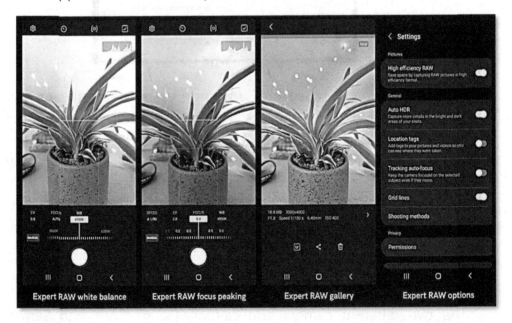

Expert RAW white balance   Expert RAW focus peaking   Expert RAW gallery   Expert RAW options

Even in the Pro mode of the Samsung camera software, you won't be able to locate the histogram tool that is included in the Expert RAW package. By using multi-frame RAW files, according to Samsung, the Expert RAW app provides a greater dynamic range than the ordinary app does. This is in comparison to the basic app.

These take a little bit longer to record and result in distinct RAW snaps from Expert RAW and Pro mode, with differing noise levels and exposure while having comparable settings. These can be captured with a digital camera. While the expert-tier software does somewhat less processing overall, it is not always possible to determine which one is objectively superior to the other.

The streamlined user interface of Expert RAW allows for easy access to the manual settings whenever they are desired or required. This is the primary benefit of using Expert RAW. It's stripped-down software that focuses only on advanced photography capabilities for professionals.

How to use Samsung Expert RAW

You will need to get familiar with all of the toggles before beginning work with the Expert RAW setting. To talk in more general terms, one of the advantages of switching to manual control is the ability to customize the camera's settings to your situation, striking a balance between the optimal exposure and your subject. After all, the camera on your phone doesn't usually capture things quite this accurately. While shooting action images, for instance, you should give importance to a rapid shutter speed, while keeping the ISO as low as possible will decrease noise and allow for more detail. **A brief description of each available choice is provided below.**

- **ISO** — Increases light capture at the expense of additional grain/noise. Increase this to allow you to set the desired shutter speed or lower it to reduce an overly bright exposure.
- **Shutter speed** — Closes the shutter faster for a sharper image at the expense of light capture. Longer shutter speeds capture more light in dim conditions but are more susceptible to blur. However, long exposure blur can create impressive light streaks and water effects.
- **EV**: This is a toggle that adjusts other auto settings in addition to providing a general exposure correction. When the value is positive, exposure is increased, whereas when the value is lower, underexposure is more likely.

- **Focus** — Use the camera's manual focusing controls to alter the focus from the foreground to the background. The focus peaking function creates a green halo around items that are in the correct focus.
- **White Balance** – The white point of your picture can be adjusted between a blue/cool (2,300K) and red/warm setting using the Kelvin (K) measurement system (10,000K). This should finish somewhere in the vicinity of the 5,000-kilobyte threshold the majority of the time.
- **Metering**: This is the process that determines which section of the picture should be used when adjusting the exposure automatically. By using centre-weighted, the camera will try to expose the subject that is located in the middle of the frame. Spot exposures are determined by a single, user-selectable point; while matrix exposures take into account the full picture's highlights and shadows.

The ability to apply significant changes to your photos is the fundamental advantage of shooting in RAW format. After you have achieved mastery in the discipline of altering exposure, the next step is to acquaint yourself with strong RAW editing software so that you can fine-tune your photographs to perfection.

Adobe's Lightroom and Google's Snapseed are two of the most well-known photo editing applications on Android. You can also transfer your photographs to a computer and editing them using Adobe Photoshop or another program of a similar kind.

Even though their capabilities differ, all of these photo editing programs provide you with the means to further improve your picture's highlights, shadows, noise, and sharpness. In addition, you will be able to experiment with different settings to adjust the colour balance and alter colours to add a creative flare to your work without having to deal with the banding and distortion difficulties that are inherent to the JPEG format.

The following is a brief illustration of one sort of picture alteration that is made feasible by using RAW.

Edit and Take Pictures with Samsung Expert RAW Using Samsung Expert RAW

- Open Expert RAW on your Samsung smartphone.
- Decide on the lens you wish to use.
- Press the shutter release button. The procedure takes some time to complete.

How to Edit RAW Images for Expert RAW

You can record RAW profiles using Expert RAW, but you need Adobe Lightroom as a third-party program to edit them. It thus accepts DNG files (compression of RAW for raw data so you can edit photos and have high-quality JPGs with lossless JPG).

- Launch **Lightroom**, and then choose the picture you wish to edit. Next, select **Profile** from the bottom Menu.
- Choose the **Galaxy RAW Profile** under **Import Profiles**.
- Browse the **GalaxyRAWProfile** after that and select to import it.
- You can use the profile after it has been imported and then apply it to your device.

CHAPTER 18

SAMSUNG CAMERA ASSISTANT APP

What is the Samsung Camera Assistant app?

You can change the Galaxy phone's default camera app settings with the Samsung Camera Assistant App. The release of the app also makes some intriguing features available.

You can adjust many features and settings using the program following your preferences. You can also use this to modify the camera app's Auto mode.

The following options and functionalities are available in the Camera Assistant app from Samsung:

- Auto HDR.
- Soften pictures.
- Auto lens switching.
- Video recording in Photo mode.
- Several pictures after the timer.
- Faster shutter.
- Camera timeout.
- Clean preview on HDMI displays.

Auto HDR: Using auto HDR, you can take photographs and movies with better details in both the light and dark regions.

The camera will focus more on the subject if HDR mode is ON. The camera will concentrate more on the backdrop while the HDR option is OFF, keeping the item visible.

[HDR Off]   [HDR On]

Soften Pictures: It softens textures and edges that are harsh in photos taken in Photo mode.

You will receive a soft picture of your skin and hair expression when it is switched ON. While it is off, you will receive photographs with rich, complex textures. Only the Picture mode and Portrait mode support the function.

Auto Lens Switching: Using the object's zoom, illumination, and distance, this feature automatically chooses the optimal lens.

To provide brilliant pictures when ON, it automatically shifts to a wide-angle lens at 3x magnification or greater. While OFF, crisp optical zoom photography is achievable with a telephoto lens at 3x magnification or more. (Notice - The outcome will be quite gloomy.)

Video Recording in Photo Mode: After enabling this mode, you can capture photos while still recording movies by pressing and holding the shutter button.

Number of Pictures after Timer: Use this option if you want to take the most photos possible of a certain situation. You can set a timer, and while it's active, you can take a maximum of 7 images at once and as few as 1. Employ it if you want a steady shot but don't want to touch the shutter button.

Faster Shutter: By taking fewer pictures, this function accelerates the shutter. Each time you push the button, a rapid-fire succession of images will appear. This will enable you to choose better photos from the ones you've recorded. (Note: The picture quality will suffer.)

Camera Timeout: This function enables you to save battery life on your smartphone. If the camera is not utilized for at least two minutes and up to ten minutes, it will automatically switch off. The time gap of 1, 2, 5, and 10 minutes may be selected in the settings for this modification.

Clean Preview on HDMI displays: You can use this option to preview on HDMI-connected screens without any settings or buttons. If the option is turned on, only the pure preview screen will be accessible when the device is connected to an external monitor.

How to download the Samsung Camera Assistant app

- You need to first download the Good Lock.
- Install it on your device.
- Download the Samsung's Camera Assistant App from the Galaxy Store.
- Install it on your device.

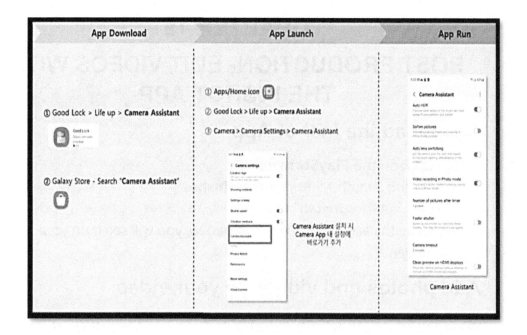

You must check the following before using the Camera Assistance app on your device:

- The Camera Assistance App won't function until you first install the Samsung Good Lock app on your smartphone. The above discussion covered how to download it.
- Your smartphone must be running One UI 5 or later, which is based on Android 13, for Samsung's Camera Assistant App to function.

CHAPTER 19
POST PRODUCTION- EDIT VIDEOS WITH THE INSHOT APP

Download the Inshot App

- Click on the **PlayStore** icon.
- On the Search Menu, type in "**Inshot**".
- Click on the "**Install**" Option.
- Once the app has been downloaded, you will see it on your Home Screen.

Add photos and videos to your video

You can create a video by merging individual video clips, photos, or both.

1. Open the **InShot application** on your smartphone. The **video, picture, and collage options** will all be shown on the home screen. Choose one of these to start with. You can combine still photos, videos, or both into a video using the **Video** option. Choose the **Picture** option from the menu if you want to edit photos. As we are now interested in video editing, choose the **Video** option.

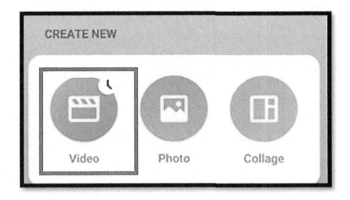

Tip: if you see a clock symbol next to the Video option, this indicates that you have drafts in the works.

2. After selecting the Video tab, use the **Create** option to begin creating a new video or editing an existing one. If you have previously altered a video in InShot, a draft of that film will display in this section. To make changes to a draft, just tap on it.

3. On the screen that opens, choose the segments of the video that you want to include in the film. You will see tabs labeled "**Video,**" "**Photo,**" **and "Everything**." To choose the photographs and videos, tap on them in the gallery. Tap the **Blank** option in the menu if you wish to begin the creation of a video from scratch. To finish, click the symbol of a green checkmark that is located at the bottom. **Tip**: To build a film only from photographs, such as a slideshow, touch on the Picture tab and pick the pictures to include in the project. The video editor screen will open where you can start editing your video.

Import other photos and videos

When you have added the first clips, you will have the option to add more clips whenever necessary should you forget to include anything. Tap the **"+" (Add)** symbol that is located on the left side of the timeline while you are on the screen for the video editor.

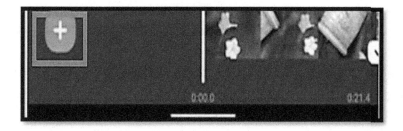

Arrange clips

The video clips have been added to the video in the order that they were added to the video, and this order is reflected on the timeline. But, you can adjust their position at any moment. To access the mode for rearranging the video clips, just touch and hold any video clip in the timeline. After that, reposition the clip thumbnail by dragging it to a new location.

Increase the timeline

You can zoom in and out of the clip previews on the video timeline by using the pinch-in and pinch-out gestures, respectively. This provides you with a clearer picture of the materials you will be dealing with.

Delete clips

Tap the specific segment you want to delete from the video, and then select it by tapping on it. You will see that it has a white margin around it. After that, choose the Delete tool from the toolbar located at the bottom of the screen.

Add effects or edits to all video clips

While you are editing clips, in general, if you hit the symbol shown as a single checkmark, any effect or modification that you make will be applied to the specific clip that you are editing. But, if you touch on the double checkmark icon instead of the single checkmark symbol, you will be able to make the update to all of the clips.

Resize video

You could want to turn a landscape video into a portrait one or vice versa, or you might want to post a movie that you published to Instagram Story on YouTube. Both of these things are possible. When this occurs, the videos will have a different aspect ratio than usual. Thus, you should alter the movies' canvas sizes rather than starting from the beginning to create them again. This is not the best method, since it may result in your video having blank borders or the video being cropped in some way.

Tap the **Canvas** option inside the InShot video editor, and then choose the desired aspect ratio from the list of available choices. To zoom in and out of the movie, use the pinching motion on your thumb and index finger. If you want to apply the new video size to the currently selected clip, press the symbol with a single checkmark; if you want to apply it to all clips, hit the icon with two checkmarks.

Change Background

After adjusting the aspect ratio of your movie, if the backdrop is white, you have the option of either filling it with colour or adding a blur effect. On Android, you can do this by selecting the Background tool from the toolbar. On an iPhone, the Background selection is located inside the Canvas tool itself. This is also the case on an iPad. Make your selection from the choices that are offered, whether it is the colour or the effect.

Tip: To make the backdrop black and then zoom out of the video so that you have black bars around it.

Crop Video

You have the option of cropping the video to the needed dimensions if you do not want the movie to have a backdrop. To do this, use the Crop tool from the toolbar. Select a dimension from the available choices, and then reposition the selection box such that it encompasses the required space. As was to be anticipated, you will miss out on some parts of the video.

Add audio from video

InShot provides some different options for adding audio to your videos. You have the option to record anything, choose music from the music library that is already incorporated into InShot, or upload a track from your local folder. To access the audio screen, you can go there by selecting the Music tool from the toolbar. To add sound to your video, go to the Tracks, Effects, or Record menu and choose the option of your choice.

Extract audio from an existing video

You can also take audio from any other video on your phone and utilize it in the video you are now shooting with InShot. Imagine that you have an Instagram reel video saved on your phone and that you want to include some of the audio from that video in the video that you are now editing. You can extract audio from videos by going into the Music app, selecting the **Tracks** option, and then tapping on the option to do so. Choose the video file to open.

Extract Audio from Current Video

You also have the option of removing the audio track from the video that you are currently editing. You will be able to alter the audio independently from the video using this. You have the option of modifying its length and volume, as well as duplicating and slicing it.

To achieve this, go to the Music tool and then touch on the video clip that is located at the very bottom of the screen. To extract the audio, choose the **Extract** option. You will then be brought to the Music screen, where you will find a distinct audio layer. To make changes, choose an item from the menu at the top.

Hint: If you are unable to download a song onto your phone, you can screen record the song while you are listening to it on YouTube or any other music app, and then utilize the option to extract audio to add the song to the video.

Removing background noise from your videos

To get rid of any audio that may already be present in your movie, go to the **Volume** tool in the toolbar and turn down the volume till it is as low as possible. To erase the audio from all clips, tap the symbol that looks like a double checkmark. Altering the volume or disabling the Music tool entirely are also options available to you while using this feature.

Add Sticker

Emojis, animated stickers, and GIFs can be added to your film with the help of the sticker tool. You can add a PNG image to your film, such as a watermark, by using the Sticker tool in Adobe Premiere Pro. To do so, touch the Sticker tool, then hit the Gallery icon at the bottom of the screen. After clicking the **Add** button, choose the picture to upload.

When it has been inserted, you can edit the length of the sticker by tapping on it in the timeline, or you can use the Edit button to add transition effects.

Customize text

To add text to your movie, choose the Text tool from the menu. You can change its hue, pattern, stroke weight, opacity, typeface, and alignment. In the screen used to change the text, you have access to all of these choices.

Even transition effects between paragraphs can be added to the text. To do so, hit the icon that is located at the very end of the Text editing toolbar. Choose the transition effect that you want. Just pick the appropriate impact for the text entering and exit by tapping on the In and Out choices, respectively.

When it has been inserted, you can adjust the length of time the text takes up by moving the boundaries of the beginning and finish points in the timeline.

Add filters and effects

To manually modify the brightness, contrast, and saturation, as well as other aspects of the image, tap on the Filter tool. You also have the option of applying filters that have already been created or adding effects such as glitch zoom, fade, and so on. After you have finished creating an effect, go to the timeline and touch on the effect to change its length.

Add a transition

To access the Transition screen, on the video timeline, hit the clock symbol that is located between the individual video segments. Choose the transition effect that you want to use.

Add multiple videos in one frame

You can create the effect of a video collage by playing many clips inside the same frame by using the PIP tool. Just add the clips you want to layer by tapping on the PIP tool and adding them.

Cut, trim, and split video

To trim, clip, or divide the video, just tap on the Pre-cut tool.

- You can remove the unwanted portions of the video from the endpoints using the Trim tool. To trim the video, drag the end edges.
- The centre section of the video is cut off using the Cut tool, and the remaining pieces are combined. To preserve the sections of the movie that you require, drag the green selection boxes.
- The Split tool enables you to divide the movie into smaller chunks, each of which functions as a separate clip. Maintain the green marker where you wish to divide the video.

Speed, Rotate, and Flip

As expected, use these tools to rotate the video, flip, or increase or decrease the speed of the video.

Tip: Split the video chunk and adjust the speed to add slow motion to that section.

Freeze Frame

You can freeze a frame with the Freeze tool for the chosen amount of time. In essence, the video will centre on the chosen frame. Press the Freeze tool while keeping the cursor on the frame you wish to freeze.

Removing watermark from videos

When editing the video, if the InShot watermark appears, press on it and watch the video commercial to get rid of it without the pro version.

Save video

To export the video after finishing editing it, hit the **Save** icon at the top. Choose the preferred frame rate and resolution before clicking the Save button. The video will be kept in the gallery on your phone.

CHAPTER 20

PHONE PHOTOGRAPHY BASICS: HOW TO TAKE GOOD PHOTOS WITH YOUR MOBILE DEVICE

Use grid lines to balance your shots

Turning on the camera's gridlines is one of the easiest and effective methods to increase the quality of your smartphone photographs. The "**rule of thirds**" is a photographic composition principle that states an image should be broken down into thirds, both horizontally and vertically, so that you have a total of nine parts. This causes a series of lines to be superimposed on the screen of the camera app on your smartphone. These lines are based on the "**rule of thirds**."

According to this theory, if you place points of interest in these intersections or along the lines, your photo will be more balanced, and level, and allow viewers to interact with it more naturally.

To activate the grid...

- Open the camera app, go to "**Settings**," scroll to the bottom of the page, and toggle the "**gridlines**" option to the "on" position.

Set your camera's focus.

Although the cameras in today's smartphones automatically concentrate on whatever is in the front of the frame when you snap a photo, not every image you take on your phone will have a clear subject. Launch the camera app on your device and press the area of the screen where you want the image to be magnified to make adjustments to where the camera lens will concentrate.

If you are trying to take a picture of something that is moving, for instance, it can be difficult for your camera to track the subject and refocus itself appropriately as required. Touch the screen to adjust the focus of your phone camera shortly before taking the image to guarantee that the moving subject is captured with the maximum amount of sharpness possible. After that, a square or circular icon will display on the screen of your camera. This will cause the focus of your photo to move to anything that is included inside the icon.

Use HDR mode.

High dynamic range, sometimes known as **HDR**, is a function available on certain camera apps that helps to bring the bright and dark aspects of a high-contrast photograph into better balance. But, its most typical use is to generate a picture that has an appearance that is analogous to what one sees with his or her own eyes. It can also be used to give images a more creative or artistic mood.

It might be challenging to get the ideal exposure for both bright and dark regions when using cameras on smartphones. You can be taking a picture of someone in a dimly lit room against a well-lit wall, or you could be taking a picture of someone outdoors in the shadow against a well-lit backdrop.

The person being shot can come out underexposed if the exposure is set to the backdrop. On the other hand, if you adjust the exposure such that it focuses on the topic, the backdrop can end up being overexposed.

HDR avoids this from happening by preserving the information in the shadows as well as the lighter and brighter regions of the image.

Use natural light.

It's not easy to discover a good smartphone shot that was taken using the flash on the device. They almost always make a photograph seem overexposed, which has the effect of distorting colours and making the subjects in the photograph appear washed out.

Even when it is dark outside, you should make use of whatever sources of natural light you can locate. This provides you with the opportunity to experiment with shadows, as seen in the second picture below, or to construct a silhouette using other sources of ambient light, such as the traffic and the buildings in the surrounding area.

When you have shot the picture, use your preferred photo editing program and experiment with the "**Exposure**" option to see if you can make the image somewhat brighter without causing it to become excessively amount of grainy.

Spend some time experimenting with the many settings and lighting possibilities available around you to take better photographs. Your photo's mood, tone, and ambiance are all affected by the lighting, therefore the more natural light you can get into it, the better. For the best results, you should avoid using the flash and instead make the most of whatever natural light is available.

Before taking a picture, you should spend some time thinking about the composition, particularly the placement of the subject with the rest of the frame, since this tends to result in the most eye-catching photographs. Your subjects should be positioned such that they are well-lit from the front, and you should try to prevent harsh artificial light from coming from the back. You should also take into account negative space, which refers to the region surrounding the topic so that it is clear that the focus should be on the subject.

Consider what you already have available to you that you might use to add some visual appeal to the shot you're taking. For instance, water can provide magnificent reflections, yet a stormy sky produces an ominous atmosphere. Keep an eye out for symmetry, recurring patterns, and leading lines; all of these elements can contribute to the creation of an excellent photograph by making the subject more visually appealing.

Adjust the camera focus

In many of the finest photographs, there is simply one fascinating subject. Hence, when you are shooting a photo of one, you need to spend some more time preparing the image. Some argue that the topic shouldn't occupy the full frame and that two-thirds of the shot should be negative space because it makes the subject shine even more.

Some expert photographers think that this helps the subject stand out even more.

- Tap the screen of your smartphone to focus the camera on your subject. This will assist to guarantee that the image is focused properly and that the lighting is optimal.

Hint: Once you have taken your picture, you can edit it with various filters and programs to make the topic even more colourful or you can crop it to frame the subject appropriately. You can also alter the photo's brightness, contrast, and saturation from your mobile device. All of these adjustments can be made in real-time.

Frame and balance your shots

One of the simplest techniques to create stunning photographs is to take images with artistically composed frames. To use the grid lines on your Galaxy camera to assist guide your shot composition, just switch on the feature. Whether you are capturing shots of your friends at a festival or working on a landscape image utilizing the rule of thirds, positioning areas of interest along the lines or intersections will guarantee that your photograph is properly balanced.

Your viewers will be able to engage with it more naturally if you divide the image into three separate parts, and this will guarantee that you generate amazing photographs that everyone can take pleasure in.

Follow the simple steps below to turn on gridlines on your Samsung Galaxy phone:

1. Open Camera app
2. Tap Settings
3. Switch and tap on Gridlines to activate
4. Tab **Back** to return to the camera screen with grid lines shown in the camera interface

Play with different perspectives

Develop your viewpoint to become more inventive. A few of the photographs with the greatest enduring impact were taken from novel and unexpected vantage points that made us reconsider how we see the world. Consider the depth, height, and angles of the situation; there is an entire universe waiting to be discovered. In addition, the unique Flex mode allows you to alter the angle at which your phone is held, allowing you to take a step back and unleash your creative side.

Don't be afraid to be creative; taking shots from a high angle can generate amazing bird's-eye views of your subject and give your photo a wonderful artistic atmosphere. Don't be scared to get creative. You can also try getting down on the ground and looking up at the world above you; you could find some very gorgeous photos. And don't forget to let your imagination go wild when it comes to choosing angles; doing so will guarantee that you can achieve a variety of effects in your photographs, giving them the perfect amount of depth and intensity.

Use a Tripod

There has never been an easy way to make sure the shot stays level and balanced when you shoot, which is especially important if you want to be in the picture and not just take a typical selfie with your arm extended. Mobile devices make it easy to take any photo on the go, but there has never been an easy way to make sure the shot stays level and balanced.

You can take rapid, hands-free photos with your smartphone by mounting it on a mobile tripod, which also frees you from the need to carry any heavy equipment with you. The majority of mobile tripods are just slightly larger than your mobile device and can bend in any direction.

Make sure your camera lens is clean

To clean the camera lens and remove any dust or particles, use a microfiber cleaning cloth that is fluffy, lint-free, and soft. It is essential to prevent any moisture from entering any openings, thus it is best to refrain from applying liquid solutions on your phone.

Keep your distance

If you go too near to the subject of your photograph, the camera won't be able to focus properly, and the resulting images will be fuzzy. Try moving farther away from the subject of your photograph; for the best results, you should be at least 30 centimetres (12 inches) away. The extraordinary Optical 10x Zoom lens found in the Galaxy S23 Ultra 5G will provide the highest quality images at a distance of 80 centimetres (32 inches).

Check the lighting

It is possible for there to be regions of underexposure and overexposure in a photograph if there is an excessive amount of light shining straight at the camera. When a photograph is underexposed, the result might be a fuzzy or blurry appearance. Your camera will automatically change the exposure to ensure that there is sufficient light, but it may struggle to focus in certain lighting conditions. As a result, you may want to try a new position or set to see whether or not this improves the quality of blurry photographs.

Your photographs can turn out fuzzy if you take them in low-light conditions. While photographing at night, it might be helpful to make use of additional sources of light, such as a ring light.

Use negative spaces

When it comes to photography, making use of "**negative space**" is an easy method to produce striking images while maintaining a spare appearance. The trick is to take pictures with big stretches of nothing in them so that the spectator is drawn into the picture.

Photographers can take three-dimensional situations and create captivating two-dimensional photos by imaginatively using both positive and negative space in their compositions. The use of negative space in photography is going to help you capture better pictures, so here's an introduction to the concept.

Understanding negative space in photography

As you are composing a picture, your attention is directed largely on the primary subject that you are attempting to capture, whether it is a mountain top in snow, a flower, or a portrait of a person.

The region that surrounds the primary topic and contributes to defining it is referred to as negative space. The empty area does not consist completely of negatives.

It might be a vast field of grass, an expanse of sky, or a body of water; nonetheless, it will typically be free of any distracting components, allowing the viewer's attention to stay fixed on the primary topic of your photograph.

Positive and negative space: What's the difference?

The primary topic of a photograph is referred to as the "**positive space**," and it is the element that the photographer hopes the audience will focus on first when they examine the image. And the region that surrounds the primary topic is referred to as the negative space. It is possible for there to be things, colours, and patterns existing in the negative space. But, they are not engaging enough to hold the viewer's attention for very long. Instead, the viewer's attention is drawn to the positive space that exists inside the photograph by the negative space.

Why is it called "negative space"?

Photographers refer to the portion of a picture that does not capture the viewer's attention as "**negative space**," which is why they use that phrase. It comprises the backdrop in your shot the majority of the time and its purpose is to support the positive space and make the composition more intriguing.

What is an example of negative space?

A buffer is created using negative space around the primary topic or subjects of your composition. The end products are often spare and emotive. One illustration of this might be a lone bird flying over a vast expanse of sky, a solitary figure standing on a deserted beach, or a lone dandelion rising above a field of verdant grass. In comparison, a photograph that does not have a lot of negative space would seem to have a lot going on in it. Imagine a large group of people attending a performance, a woods packed with trees, or a picture of someone that fills the picture frame.

How does negative space affect photography?

The viewer's attention is drawn to the topic at the same time as the drama and mystery created by negative space are enhanced.

The spectator can experience feelings of tranquillity, or even isolation depending on the effect that the photograph's negative space has on them. When there is more space in a photograph, viewers are more likely to have a strong emotional response.

Why is negative space important?

Your topic will be brought to the forefront of the composition with the assistance of negative space, which helps declutter it. Experimenting with the diverse feelings that different arrangements of objects might elicit is made much easier by using it.

A picture that was taken against a cluttered backdrop is often less compelling than one that included a lot of space in the background.

How to create negative space in your photos

Composition is the single most important factor to think about when trying to generate negative space in your photographs. While using your Samsung, it is simple to take pictures without paying any regard to the amount of positive or negative space in the frame.

For a photograph to effectively make use of negative space, the photographer has to take their time and focus intently on the subject of the shot before clicking the shutter.

Here are a few pointers that might help you create stunning photographs by making use of the "**negative space**."

1. Use a cardboard frame to help you visualize the space

This method is often used by painters as a means of assisting them in visualizing or composing a scene; but, it is just as helpful for photographers.

Construct a miniature picture frame out of cardboard with an opening that approximately corresponds to the aspect ratio of a typical image.

The dimensions of three inches by five inches are ideal for the majority of uses.

You can utilize the frame to assist you to adapt any three-dimensional picture into a two-dimensional one that is worthy of being photographed before you take the shot.

This not only makes it much simpler to perceive the space surrounding your subject, but it's also a fantastic tool for learning various compositional strategies.

2. Create negative space in front of moving objects or people

Every photograph you take has a narrative, and it is your responsibility as a photographer to frame your shots in such a manner that the narrative emerges from the picture. It is vital to remember to leave some space in front of your subject while photographing animals, people, or moving objects. This allows the viewer to imagine the subject moving through the environment as they are looking at the photograph.

When you are taking pictures of an automobile, you should make sure that there is enough room in front of the vehicle so that the spectator can easily imagine what is happening. Both humans and animals have these characteristics. Give them room to express the direction they are traveling toward or the direction they are gazing at.

3. Use Portrait mode to blur the background

While taking pictures of individuals, this function was developed to assist photographers in producing an impression of depth of field in their photographs. The backdrop is blurred while using the Portrait mode, which helps the subject of the photograph stand out from its surroundings. You can utilize the Portrait mode to blur a backdrop that might otherwise be a potential distraction for the viewer if you are constructing a photo with negative space. You can generate the appearance of negative space with this technique, which is useful even in crowded areas.

4. Practice with more than one subject in a single scene

When you first begin to play with negative space, you will most likely centre your attention on a single thing to serve as the primary point of interest. But, after you have gained a better understanding of this idea and feel more at ease with it, you will be able to discuss more than one topic. It is not unusual for a single photograph to include two or more subjects at the same time. The key is to strike a healthy equilibrium between the amount of positive and negative space in the frame while at the same time ensuring that the primary topics occupy the majority of the space.

5. Find a balance between positive and negative space

Since the presence of negative space has the effect of making your photographs seem, sparer, striking a balance between the many elements of the scene is of even more significance. Experimentation and practice are two of the finest ways to learn how to get the outcomes you want out of a composition. Numerous elements inside a piece can cause the balance to alter ever-so-slightly.

You may need to make adjustments to the size of the focal point inside the frame, the proportion of highlights to shadows, and the location of positive space within the background to achieve greater balance within your picture. When trying to achieve a feeling of equilibrium inside an image, it is sometimes sufficient to simply add or remove negative space.

6. Try experimenting with black and white to accentuate negative space

Using monochromatic editing methods may often help photographs with negative space seem more interesting. Your picture will seem cleaner as a result of using a black-and-white filter, which will allow the viewer to focus more intently on your composition.

You can take your shot using a third-party camera app that supports shooting in black and white, or you can edit your photo using post-processing software that includes a black-and-white filter.

7. Let your imagination rule the shot

The most important thing to keep in mind while searching for the ideal photo is to utilize your imagination and creativity.

Anybody can take a picture, but producing art is accomplished by paying close attention to the positive and negative space in a situation and using it in a way that compels the viewer to want to know more.

Does negative space have to be black or white?

Never in a million years! Within the realm of design, the words "**negative space**" and **"white space"** are synonymous with one another and are used interchangeably. When it comes to photography, however, "**negative space**" refers to any area of the frame that does not divert the attention of the spectator away from the primary subject of the composition. It can have colour and texture, and it is also possible for it to have forms and things. The objective is to produce a picture in which the absence of something serves to emphasize rather than detract from the presence of something wonderful.

Negative space photography is a terrific method to learn and develop as a photographer, especially if you truly want to practice constructing intriguing situations. Getting rid of the clutter compels you to search for drama and emotion in the way your subject engages with the space that is now available to them.

Find different points of view

Shooting photographs from an unusual or unanticipated perspective can make them more memorable; this technique often results in the creation of an illusion of depth or height with the objects in the photographs. Since the vast majority of pictures taken with mobile devices are shot either head-on or from above, this feature helps the image stand out even more.

You can try shooting a picture looking straight up and using the sky as a kind of negative space, as seen in the first picture down below. Instead, you may attempt to take it at a somewhat downward angle.

Experiment with Reflections

The sight of the sky reflected in a body of water has always struck me as particularly picturesque. Our eyes are naturally attracted to reflections, which is one of the reasons why we like seeing things like that so much. Hence, search for picture situations in which you may interact with them.

Reflections can be found in a wide variety of unexpected settings, including puddles, bigger bodies of water, mirrors, eyeglasses, drinking glasses, and metallic surfaces, to name just a few.

Use Guidelines

Certain photographs have a line that directs the attention of the viewer to a particular portion of the picture frame. These lines are referred to as leading lines. Consider stairways, building facades, railroad lines, roadways, or even a walk through the woods; they may be linear or curved in their configuration.

Even if you simply managed to stumble across a very interesting form by chance, adding leading lines to your shot may make it appear like it was carefully planned. This is because leading lines are wonderful for generating a feeling of depth in an image.

Look for symmetry

The majority of the guidelines that we apply to compose effective images originate from traditional forms of art. The techniques that the great artists of painting employed to create their works hundreds of years ago are still relevant to your photography now, just as they were back then. The fundamentals of translating the three-dimensional world into a two-dimensional canvas remain the same.

The concept of symmetry is one of these essential concepts. When it comes to photography, using symmetry and patterns are excellent strategies to make your photographs more visually attractive and powerful.

When elements of your composition mirror one another, this is an example of symmetry. As you consider the human body, you'll see that it possesses vertical symmetry. The right half is reflected in its left counterpart. Suppose you have taken a photo and then folded it in half down the centre. If both halves of the picture are the same, then we may say that it is symmetrical.

As you begin to seek it, you will discover that symmetry is present in every aspect of nature. The majority of things that have been created by humans also exhibit symmetry. Many of the things that we use daily, like automobiles, aircraft, boats, ships, homes, and other structures, all have symmetry.

Why? Because the human brain is naturally drawn to appreciate symmetrical things. When we think of beauty, symmetry is often the first thing that comes to mind.

Since it is not difficult to harness this virtually natural and gorgeous composition approach, a lot of artists employ it. This is one reason why. The use of symmetry is ubiquitous across the artistic world, and its practitioners range from painters and sculptors to architects and photographers.

In the field of photography, several notable instances can be found in the area of wedding photography. Why do pictures of the wedding party standing in a row next to the bride and groom during a wedding seem to be so popular? Symmetry. What about the church's seats lined up in rows, or even some images of the aisle with the various decorations? This is another example of symmetry.

Pay attention to the repeating pattern

When powerful visual components, such as lines, geometric shapes, forms, and colors, are repeated over and over again, such as in a pattern, the result is a very aesthetically beautiful pattern known as a repetitive pattern. These patterns can have a powerful effect on the viewer's perception, and sometimes all it takes to produce an arresting picture is a snapshot of something as simple as a beautifully tiled floor. On other occasions, it is more entertaining to keep a lookout for places where they arise organically or inadvertently, as is the case with the congruent fire escapes on the left.

Experiment with colour blocking

Isn't it awesome when a photograph is entirely monochromatic except for one specific detail? It has come to our attention that yes, in fact, there are applications available for doing that. One of our faves is called **Touch Colour**, and it's an app that takes a photo, turns it into grayscale, and then allows you to colour in the sections of the image that you want to colorize.

The use of colour blocking is a technique that can be used to draw attention to certain aspects of a photograph, such as a vividly coloured plant or object, for example. It accomplishes an objective similar to that of negative space in that it can assist a particular subject to stand out; but, with colour blocking, the photo's other parts stay intact, resulting in a picture that is consistent throughout.

Don't Zoom in

While taking a picture from a faraway vantage point, the temptation to zoom in on a particular aspect of what you're attempting to capture is always there. Nevertheless, it is recommended that you should not zoom close on the picture since doing so might cause it to seem grainy, fuzzy, or pixelated.

Instead, you should make an effort to approach closer to your subject — unless it is a dangerous animal, in which case we would suggest maintaining your distance — or shoot the shot from a pre-set distance, then trim it later on if necessary. This way, you won't have to worry about sacrificing quality, and it will be much simpler to manipulate or optimize a bigger picture.

Capture small details.

You may be familiar with the proverb that says, "**It's the little things**."." It may sometimes be the case with photographs as well. It's possible to create highly interesting visual material by using close-up photography that focuses on capturing minute, detailed, and delicate elements. Always be on the lookout for different surface textures and patterns, such as paint that is chipping, a gravel road, or a tile table top.

Pro Tip: Use the "**sharpen**" tool in your favourite photo editing app to (conservatively) sharpen the details of your photo.

Use Flash only during the day

A picture could turn out better if you use the flash on your camera, but doing so at night is quite unlikely to be beneficial. Since dark photos expose a much more pronounced contrast against the light emitted by your phone's flash, this may cause any flash to seem intrusive and uneven.

But, even in areas that have enough lighting, using a flash may serve to diffuse the harsh light cast by the primary subject behind them or below them.

Look for shadows on the ground or against vertical surfaces when you frame your next photo. You may want to crop out any shadows that are too dark. If you see any, manually turn on the flash in the camera app on your device. It is not certain that your phone will detect the shadows that you wish to get rid of even if you set the camera flash on your phone to the "**auto**" setting. Make sure you don't forget to turn the flash off after you're through using it. The next time you're taking product photography, give some thought to the significance of flash and how it might be used to highlight or hide specific lines and details.

Adjust the exposure manually in the camera app

Another component of your smartphone camera that requires manual adjustment is the exposure setting. While the camera app on your phone is active, tapping the screen will not only cause the lens to refocus on a new subject, but it will also cause the camera to make an automated adjustment to the amount of light it allows. Even this won't always look the way you want it to. It is preferable to adjust by hand. Launch the camera app on your device, and then press anywhere on the screen to manually adjust the exposure settings. As the lens refocuses, you'll see a vertical scale and a very little sun symbol appear on the screen. To alter the brightness, just make a slow swiping motion with your finger up and down this scale.

Create abstracts.

Photos that are considered abstract are those that are intended to convey the essence of an item or sequence of objects without showing the complete environment as a whole. To put it another way, their function is to serve the objective of producing one-of-a-kind and unexpected photographs from mundane situations. This effect can be achieved by either cutting off an abstract area of an otherwise ordinary photograph or by shooting close-up photographs of things in such a way that the spectator is left wondering – with appreciation, of course — what the subject of the photograph might be. In addition, things that has patterns or repetition provide excellent candidates for abstract photography, such as the sliced figs seen in the following image.

Capturing Candids

Photos that have been posed may be quite useful for remembering joyful times spent with family and friends, as well as the odd chance encounter with a famous person. Yet, candid images of people doing things or individuals with other people may sometimes be significantly more engaging than staged ones.

The reason for this is that candid photographs are superior in terms of their ability to capture the feeling and spirit of a particular moment.

Just taking as many photographs as you can is one of the most effective strategies for obtaining an image of this kind. You'll have more options to choose from, and the best photos usually occur when, to use a metaphor, all the "**stars align**" in a single moment: everyone's eyes are open, one person is tilting their head just so, and you finally got a shot of your friend who smiles with his teeth when his lips are closed.

Be Eccentric

A fantastic photograph is defined not only by its composition but also by the subject matter that it depicts. Creative, one-of-a-kind concepts may give rise to some of the most fun and astonishing photographs.

When it comes to eliciting feelings in your audience, images are much more powerful than words; hence, you should strive to have your photographs convey a message.

You should try to think creatively about what you are recording since the people who examine your work could be pleasantly surprised by an interesting or unusual topic.

Force them to laugh

In relation to evoking feelings, the photographs that make us laugh are often the ones that stick in our minds the longest. It's humorous because it's unexpected, but there's also a part of us that admires the elderly lady in the picture below who is wearing a brightly coloured blouse that says "**Hello hater**."

The second picture makes fun of the traditional food images that are popular on Instagram by depicting a dog toy on a plate, but it does it from the point of view of the dog.

It is far more probable that your viewers will love your shot if you can make them chuckle.

Clean the cell phone lens

A camera on a smartphone may be easier to carry about than a full-fledged camera designed for a photojournalist, but that convenience comes at the expense of protection.

When you leave the home, your phone is most likely tucked away in one of your pockets or your bag. The camera lens of the gadget is continuously accumulating a wide variety of particles, including lint and dust. Before you take a picture with this lens, be sure to wipe it off with a clean, soft cloth. It's possible that you won't be able to determine how filthy the lens was until you begin editing your photo; thus, checking that the lens is spotless before you take a picture will save you from having to start over from the beginning.

Attach an external lens.

Do you want to seem refined? External lenses are for you. There are quite a few available that can be mounted to the top of your smartphone's main camera lens. These add-ons, which range from fish-eye lenses to wide-angle lenses, may give your photographs an altogether new quality and point of view.

Edit your images

The act of composing and shooting the picture with your smartphone is simply the beginning of the process of making it aesthetically interesting. The next stage, which is also a very important one, consists of editing your photographs. When it comes to photography, filters may be a very helpful tool, especially for achieving one of two objectives: **1)** removing flaws from an image or 2**)** making food seem even tastier to the viewer. The use of beauty filters is a frequent quick remedy, and the Samsung photo app now includes several filters that are comparable. There are other applications like **Photo** that may automatically repair face photographs without requiring a significant amount of manual labour. And what about those pictures of your everyday fare that you post online? Foodie is one of the most recent applications that can be downloaded, and it has its collection of filters that are tailored to various kinds of cuisine.

Shoot better pictures

We are now able to snap photographs of a high standard and edit them with a minimum of bells and whistles on the same mobile device that we use for making phone calls. This is made possible by the editing applications that come preinstalled on our mobile devices.

Conclusion

In conclusion, the Samsung Galaxy S23 Series is one of the best smartphones, with it exceptional camera array, solid performance, and beautiful design, it is an excellent choice for those looking for a new Android smartphone, offering improved low-light performance, with images rivalling even some of the best phones out there in the market.

"Thanks for reading this book. If you enjoyed this book, please consider leaving an honest review."

INDEX

1

10 xs Telephoto, 11, 18
12-megapixel images, 2

2

200-megapixel sensor, 3

3

3x optical zoom lens, 3

5

50-megapixel shooting option, 2
50MP mode, 12
50MP primary sensor, 12

8

8K video, 69, 71
8K Video Recording, 69
8K Video Recording and Editing, 69

A

A bright red bar, 41
A camera on a smartphone, 117
A timer symbol, 14
a wide-angle lens, 2, 87
about "**time-lapse**" on smartphones, 38
access a larger universe, 81
access the app screen, 28
access the **Camera** app, 6
access your applications, 6
access your apps, 29, 31, 41
Activate or Deactivate a Timer, 41
activate **Smart View**, 71

Add a transition, 96
Add audio from video, 93
Add colour, 55
Add effects or edits to all video clips, 92
Add multiple videos, 96
Add multiple videos in one frame, 96
Add photos and videos, 90
Add photos and videos to your video, 90
Add Sticker, 95
adding music, 64
additional alternatives, 53
Additional features, 8
additional frames, 39
additional info, 29
Additional tools, 59
Additional tools for editing, 59
Additional tools for editing photos, 59
Additional tools for editing photos/videos, 59
Adjust aspect ratio, 59
Adjust background effect intensity, 22
Adjust the camera focus, 101
Adjust the focus to capture, 32
Adjust the focus to capture details, 32
adjusts the shutter speed, 13
Adobe Premiere Rush, 59, 60
Advanced Features, 5
amazing appearance, 31
amazing picture, 49
amazing picture feature, 49
amazing picture feature known as AR Zone, 49
among content producers, 64
an AR emoji, 51
an excellent choice, 119
Android smartphone, 119
Animals, 79
animated stickers, 95
Anyone nearby, 48
Aperture & Shutter Speed, 33
App from the Galaxy, 88
app's standout features, 64
AR, 49, 50, 51, 52, 76

AR (Augmented Reality) Emoji, 76
AR Doodle, 49, 50
AR Emoji, 49, 50, 51, 52, 76
AR Emoji Camera, 49, 50
AR Emoji Stickers, 49, 50, 51, 52
AR Emoji Studio, 49, 50, 51
AR emojis as profile pictures, 49
AR stickers, 50
AR Zone, 49, 50, 51, 52
Arrange clips, 91
arrangement of the elements, 19
AR-related features, 49
arrow icon, 42
arrow pointing down, 25
Astrophoto, 14
Astrophoto mode, 14
astrophotography option, 14
Attach an external lens., 117
audio mixing, 61
Augmented Reality, 76
Auto Framing, 19, 20, 21
Auto HDR, 86
Auto HDR., 86
Auto Lens Switching, 87
Auto lens switching., 86
Auto-generate stories, 47
automated super steady, 7
automated super steady feature, 7
Available options, 33

B

background noise, 8, 94
Backlight, 77
Backlit, 79
basketball court, 35
Be Eccentric, 116
Beaches, 79
beautiful design, 119
beginner photographer, 19
Big circle, 22
bigger screen, 1
Bluetooth, 29
Blur, 22, 59, 77
bottom menu, 44

bottom of the image, 7
bottom of the screen, 6, 13, 24, 40, 44, 46, 51, 58, 59, 70, 71, 77, 82, 92, 94, 95
bottom right corner, 5, 11, 22
bottom right-hand corner, 14
bottom-right corner of the screen, 16
brighter, 3, 8, 32, 99, 100
brightness for footage, 1
brightness for footage captured at 4K 60fps, 1
By tapping, 52

C

camera app, 5, 76, 80, 81, 86, 109
camera array, 2
Camera Assistant, 86, 88, 89
Camera Assistant app, 86, 88
Camera program, 5
camera software, 2, 13, 80, 82
Camera Timeout, 88
Camera timeout., 86
camera's focus, 3, 99
camera's focus lock, 3
camera's focus lock onto elements, 3
capture button, 22, 30, 78, 79
capture footage, 1
Capture option, 19
Capture small details., 114
Capturing Candids, 116
capturing video, 7, 60
Cat, 79
Centre Stage, 20
chain fast food restaurant, 32
Change Background, 93
Change background effect., 78
Change icon, 73
CHANGE THE COLOR TONE, 15
CHANGE THE COLOR TONE FOR SELFIES, 15
change the resolution to, 69, 70
Change theme, 72
Check the lighting, 103
choose **Albums**, 44, 45
Choose Camera, 31, 41
Choose Camera., 31

Choose **Edit**, 44
Choose MODE or swipe across the screen, 41, 42
choose MORE PRO or PRO VIDEO, 33
Choose Panorama, 30
choose the astrophoto, 14
choose the astrophoto icon, 14
choose the Create button, 45
Choose the desired speed, 41
Choose the **Galaxy RAW Profile** under **Import Profiles.**, 85
choose the **Magic wand**, 16
choose the **Magic wand** symbol, 16
Choose the preferred background effect, 22
choose the preview thumbnail., 30
Choose **Video**, 67
choose VIDEO from the menu, 18
Choosing the Right 'Lapse, 40
chroma keying, 61, 64, 66
Clean Preview on HDMI displays, 88
Clean preview on HDMI displays., 86
Clean the cell phone lens, 117
Click on the **PlayStore** icon, 90
close-up, 27, 114, 115
Clothing, 79
Cloud, 29
collection of filters, 118
Colorpoint, 23
colour correction, 60, 61
Colour mix, 56, 57
colour range, 33
combining in addition, 66
computational techniques, 19
Conclusion, 119
condense the progression of motion, 38
Contacts only, 48
Control the System volume, 9
crafted Spotify playlists, 8
Create a narrative, 47
Create abstracts., 115
Create album, 44, 45
Create an album, 45
create films, 65
Create Stories, 47

crescent moon, 7, 11, 18
Crop video, 58
Crop Video, 93
Customize text, 95
CUSTOMIZE THEMES, 72
CUSTOMIZE THEMES AND ICONS, 72
Customize your My Emoji, 50
Customize your My Emoji avatar, 50
Cut, 96
Cut, trim, and split video, 96
cutting, 7, 65, 66, 115
cutting-edge nightography, 7
cutting-edge nightography features, 7

D

Deco Image, 52
Deco Photo, 49
Deco Pic, 50, 52
Delete AR emoji stickers, 52
Delete clips, 92
Delete icon, 74
Delete photos and videos, 45
Depending on the emoji, 50
desktop pro, 65
Different ways to take pictures, 9
digital zoom, 4, 79
dim conditions, 83
DIRECTOR VIEW AND DUAL RECORDING, 24
Director's View, 24, 52, 53
DIRECTOR'S VIEW, 24, 53
DNG files, 85
Dog, 79
Done button, 45, 54, 67
Don't Zoom in, 113
Double press, 5
Download icon, 72
Download theme, 72
drawing icon., 50
Drink, 79
DSLRs or modern mirrorless, 2
DSLRs or modern mirrorless cameras, 2
Dual recording, 24, 26, 53
Dual recording function, 26
dual recording mode, 24

Dual-recorded vlogs, 53
dynamic range, 1, 3, 80, 82, 99

E

EDIT, 54, 69, 90
EDIT PHOTOS, 54
EDIT PHOTOS AND VIDEOS, 54
Edit video speed, 58
Edit your images, 118
editing of 4K videos, 62
editing option, 54, 55
editing options, 54, 57, 63, 69
editing your photographs., 118
Email, 29
emoji sticker, 52
Emojis, 95
employment of extra noise-reduction, 2
employment of extra noise-reduction processing., 2
employs 2x2 pixel groups, 3
ENABLE SCENE OPTIMIZER, 12
Enable the feature, 47
enhanced focusing technique, 3
Erase button at the bottom, 74
EV, 80, 81, 83
exaggerated appearance, 2
exceptional camera array, 119
Experiment with colour blocking, 113
Experiment with Reflections, 110
Expert RAW, 14, 80, 81, 82, 83, 85
Expert RAW from Samsung's Galaxy, 81
Exposure, 33, 100
Extract Audio, 94
Extract audio from an existing video, 94
Extract Audio from Current Video, 94
Eyeblink, 77

F

Face effects, 54
Fast Motion, 76
Faster Shutter, 88
Faster shutter., 86
favourite option, 64

fewer megapixels, 1
filming in the fluorescent, 36
filming in the fluorescent or flickering light, 36
filming vistas, 2
Filmora, 62
filters, 59, 60, 62, 63, 65, 66, 95, 101, 118
Find different points of view, 110
finest image, 19, 27
Flaw detection, 77
Flip video, 58
Floating Shutter Button, 10
Focus, 32, 78, 84
Foodie, 118
Force them to laugh, 116
Frame and balance your shots, 101
Frames, 52
Freeze Frame, 97
front and rear lenses, 11
full resolution of 50MP, 12
full-resolution, 2
full-resolution images, 2

G

Galaxy Camera, 5, 10
Galaxy Camera., 5
Galaxy RAW Profile, 85
Galaxy S23, 1, 3, 5, 6, 7, 8, 9, 12, 13, 14, 15, 16, 19, 20, 28, 31, 32, 40, 69, 103, 119
Galaxy S23 and S23 Plus, 1
Galaxy S23 or S23 Plus, 1
Galaxy Store, 9, 46, 67, 81, 88
GalaxyRAWProfile, 85
Gallery settings, 46
GIFs, 8, 52, 95
Glitch, 23
Gmail, 29
Go to the VIDEO menu, 69
Good food, 31
Good food deserves Food mode, 31
GoPro camera, 63
GoPro family, 40
gorgeous composition approach, 112
gray square, 36

Great photos, 32
Great photos in any lighting, 32
Greenery, 79
Group albums, 45
group-able pixels, 3

H

HDMI-connected screens, 88
high level of detail, 15
higher chance of capturing, 14
hit the setting icon, 13
hold the emoji symbol, 50, 52
How to Edit RAW Images, 85
How to Edit RAW Images for Expert, 85
How to look at pictures, 43
HOW TO MAKE USE OF SINGLE TAKE, 27
How to Set a Video as Your Lock Screen Wallpaper, 66
HOW TO TAKE GOOD PHOTOS, 98
HOW TO TAKE GOOD PHOTOS WITH YOUR MOBILE DEVICE, 98
HOW TO USE HYPERLAPSE, 38
HOW TO USE HYPERLAPSE/TIMELAPSE, 38
HOW TO USE PRO MODE, 33
HOW TO USE PRO MODE OR PRO VIDEO, 33
HOW TO USE PRO MODE OR PRO VIDEO MODE, 33
HOW TO USE PRO MODE OR PRO VIDEO MODE ON YOUR GALAXY, 33
HOW TO USE PRO MODE OR PRO VIDEO MODE ON YOUR GALAXY PHONE, 33
HOW TO USE PRO MODE OR PRO VIDEO MODE ON YOUR GALAXY PHONE Pro, 33
HOW TO USE PRO MODE OR PRO VIDEO MODE ON YOUR GALAXY PHONE Pro Video, 33
How to Use the Power Button, 5
Hyperlapse, 38, 39, 40, 41, 42, 76
hyperlapse appear decent, 39
hyperlapse of a vacation, 40

I

images and videos, 8, 33, 47
images rivalling, 119
Import other photos and videos, 91
Important note, 11, 18
improved 8K 30 frames per second, 1
improved low-light performance, 119
including Ultra Wide, 53
Increase the timeline, 92
INCREASE TIMER IN NIGHT MODE, 13
Indoor scenes, 79
Inshot, 62, 90
InShot, 63, 90, 91, 92, 93, 94, 97
Instagram, 1, 63, 64, 65, 66, 92, 94, 117
installation, 3
INTRODUCTION, 1
Introduction to Super Slow-Mo, 35
ISO, 33, 34, 80, 81, 83

J

JPEG files, 3

K

Keep your distance, 103
keep your phone steady while filming., 7
Kelvin (K) measurement system, 84
keyframe animation, 61
keyframe animations, 64
kinds of cuisine, 118
Kinemaster, 60

L

launch the camera, 5, 12, 14, 15, 31, 40
Launch the **camera app**, 13, 15, 16, 29, 99, 115
Launch **Wonderland**, 67
LED lights, 37
lens sensors, 11, 19
Lens smudge, 77
less image noise, 3
light circumstances, 2
Lightroom, 80, 84, 85
Lightroom or Photoshop, 80
Live focus, 78
LIVE FOCUS, 22

LIVE FOCUS ON YOUR GALAXY, 22
LIVE FOCUS ON YOUR GALAXY SMARTPHONE, 22
Live Focus/Portrait Mode, 78
locked screen, 5
Longer shutter, 83
Longer shutter speeds, 83
Longer shutter speeds capture, 83
Longer shutter speeds capture more light, 83
Look for symmetry, 111
lossless JPG, 85
low light conditions, 3
LumaFusion, 61, 62

M

Magisto, 65
Main camera, 2
Main features of the camera, 6
Main features of the camera app, 6
Make sure your camera lens is clean, 103
making phone calls, 118
making waves, 1
manual camera features, 80
Manual Focus, 33
Manual settings, 80
MASK, 50
Masks, 52
MASTERING THE S23 CAMERA, 5
MASTERING THE S23 CAMERA APP, 5
Messages, 29, 52
Metering, 84
minimum of bells, 118
MIRROR, 50
mobile device, 7, 60, 101, 102, 118
More options, 44, 45, 47, 55, 56, 57, 70
most recent applications, 118
motion picture, 38
motion tracking, 61, 62
motion tracking, colour, 61
motion tracking, colour correction, 61
Move photos and videos to albums, 44
movement shots, 8
moving images automatically, 15

Multi-camera standby, 52
multicolored static, 23
multi-track editing, 61
mysterious appearance, 22

N

negative space, 100, 101, 103, 104, 105, 106, 107, 108, 109, 110, 113
new camera upgrades, 1
New Features of the S23 series Camera, 6
New Features of the S23 series Camera app, 6
NEW LEVEL OF SLOW MOTION, 35
NEW LEVEL OF SLOW MOTION WITH GALAXY PHONE, 35
NEW LEVEL OF SLOW MOTION WITH GALAXY PHONE SUPER SLOW, 35
NEW LEVEL OF SLOW MOTION WITH GALAXY PHONE SUPER SLOW MOTION, 35
night mode, 13, 14
Night portrait, 6
Night Portrait, 11, 18
Night portrait and Night selfie, 6
Night Portrait feature, 11
Night scenes, 79
Night selfie films, 7
Night video, 7
Night video and Night selfie, 7
Night video and Night selfie video, 7
Nightography, 6, 32
nighttime, 11
Number of Pictures after Timer, 88

O

Object eraser, 54
Object Image, 11, 18
Object image stabilization, 18
Object Image Stabilization, 11, 18
objects, 3, 21, 36, 106, 107, 110, 115
one bigger pixel, 2
one sort of picture alteration, 85
Open Camera app, 102
Open the app, 33
open the camera, 76
Open up **Good Lock**, 67

Open Video Editor, 57
operating system, 76
optical zoom, 3, 4, 69, 87
Optimized scenes include Food, 79
original shutter position, 10

P

palm facing the screen, 10
panorama mode, 30
parameters, 26, 46, 79
part of the photos holding the food, 32
Pay attention to the repeating pattern, 112
People, 79
PHONE PHOTOGRAPHY, 98
PHONE PHOTOGRAPHY BASICS, 98
phone's camera, 50
photo mode, 13
photographic skills., 19
photographs, 2, 3, 6, 8, 9, 12, 13, 18, 21, 32, 33, 38, 39, 43, 44, 45, 46, 47, 50, 65, 70, 80, 84, 86, 87, 91, 98, 100, 101, 102, 103, 106, 107, 108, 109, 110, 111, 114, 115, 116, 118
photograph's composition, 19
photography, 3, 11, 15, 31, 39, 80, 83, 87, 103, 104, 105, 109, 110, 111, 112, 114, 115, 118
Picture mode., 12
Picture-in-picture, 25, 53
Picture-in-Picture, 66
PIN, 5
pinching the screen, 7
PIP, 53, 66, 96
pixel binning, 2, 3
PLAY, 50
Play with different perspectives, 102
Please note, 5, 77, 78, 79
PORTRAIT, 11, 18, 22
portrait-mode photos, 3
Portraits, 79
POST PRODUCTION-, 90
PowerDirector, 60, 61
predecessors' 10-megapixel, 1
predecessors' 10-megapixel selfie, 1
predecessors' 10-megapixel selfie cameras, 1
preinstalled on our mobile devices, 118
press the **Download** symbol, 25
press the Save button, 44, 71
Press the Volume key, 9
previous configuration, 12
primary camera, 4
prior Galaxy Ultra phones, 4
Purchased items, 74

Q

quadruple back camera system, 3
Quick Launch, 5
Quick launch camera, 5
Quick Share, 47, 48
Quik, 63

R

RAW file format, 81
raw files, 3
RAW for raw data, 85
RAW snaps, 83
RECORD, 69
record a selfie video, 8
Record button, 7, 18, 26, 35, 36, 53, 70
record in Super Slow-mo., 36
Record more simultaneously with Director View, 24
Record more simultaneously with Director View & Dual, 24
Record more simultaneously with Director View & Dual Recording, 24
record RAW profiles, 85
Record video, 28
record videos, 52, 82
RECORD, EDIT, AND SHARE 8K VIDEO ON GALAXY PHONE, 69
recording a video, 26
rectangle symbol, 24
Remove theme, 74
Removing watermark from videos, 97
Resize video, 92

resolution of 12 megapixels, 12, 15
resolution of 40 megapixels, 1
Restore purchased themes, 74
Rotate, 58, 96
Rotate video, 58

S

Samsung, 1, 2, 3, 12, 13, 14, 15, 19, 20, 21, 28, 29, 31, 40, 49, 50, 51, 52, 66, 67, 74, 80, 81, 82, 83, 85, 86, 88, 89, 101, 106, 118, 119
Samsung account, 81
SAMSUNG CAMERA, 86
SAMSUNG CAMERA ASSISTANT, 86
SAMSUNG CAMERA ASSISTANT APP, 86
Samsung Expert RAW, 80, 85
SAMSUNG GALAXY, 12
SAMSUNG GALAXY S23, 12
SAMSUNG GALAXY S23 CAMERA, 12
SAMSUNG GALAXY S23 CAMERA TIPS, 12
Samsung phones, 2
Samsung phones defaults, 2
Samsung photo app, 118
Samsung's Expert Raw, 3
Samsung's Expert Raw software, 3
Samsung's high-end flagship, 3
Samsung's high-end flagship model, 3
Save video, 59, 97
SCENE, 12, 50
Scene Optimiser, 78, 79
Scene Optimiser feature, 78
Scene Optimizer, 13, 78
Scene Optimizer function, 13
Scene optimizer on, 79
scheme, 5
scientific applications, 39
Search Menu, 90
second telephoto lens, 4
select **SINGLE TAKE**, 27
Select the Settings option., 5, 9
selecting AR Emoji, 76
selecting the right white balance, 33
selection box, 93
Selfie mode, 15

sensitive the camera, 33
series of phones, 20
Set a photo or video, 66
Set a photo or video as wallpaper, 66
Set a Video as Your Home Screen, 67
Set a Video as Your Home Screen Wallpaper, 67
Setting a video, 67
Setting a video as your Home screen, 67
Settings, 5, 9, 29, 47, 98, 102
settings in addition, 83
several options to customize, 57
Several pictures after the timer., 86
SHARE 8K VIDEO, 69
SHARE 8K VIDEO ON GALAXY, 69
Share photos and videos, 47
sharp details, 6
sharpness of the colours, 23
Shoe, 79
shoot a selfie, 10
Shoot better, 118
Shoot better pictures, 118
Shooting, 9, 11, 110
shooting a video, 26
Shooting methods, 9
shooting perspective, 31
shooting settings, 76
short amount of time, 63, 65
Shotcut, 66
ShotCut, 66
ShotCut is a powerful video, 66
ShotCut is a powerful video editor, 66
ShotCut is a powerful video editor and creator, 66
Show palm, 10
shutter button, 9, 10, 15, 19, 27, 41, 78, 87, 88
shutter faster for a sharper image, 83
Shutter speed, 83
Side key, 5
significant amount, 118
significant amount of manual labour, 118
significant camera enhancements, 3
single film, 35
Single symbol, 25

Single Take, 15, 27, 28
Single Take feature, 15
Size and format, 71
Sky, 79
slow-motion, 3, 36, 63
smartphone, 10, 13, 19, 20, 21, 31, 47, 68, 76, 85, 88, 89, 90, 98, 100, 101, 102, 114, 117, 118
Smoothness, 54
snap a selfie, 6, 31
snap high-resolution, 70
snap high-resolution 33MP, 70
snap photographs, 118
Snow, 79
So, what does each camera do?, 2
Soften Pictures, 87
Soften pictures., 86
software, 19, 39, 61, 63, 64, 65, 80, 81, 82, 83, 84, 109
solid performance, 119
SOME FEATURES, 12
SOME FEATURES YOU SHOULD TRY, 12
Speaking of video, 1
specified a locking mechanism, 5
Speed, 96
Speed, Rotate, and Flip, 96
Splice, 64, 65
Spot colour, 55
Spot exposures, 84
Stage, 79
Stamps, 52
Standard, 33
standard timelapse, 40
star trails, 14
start **Night shoot**, 7
start recording, 7, 18, 26
Start the camera., 5, 9
stop recording, 26, 51, 53
Storyblocks Library, 61
stunningly high quality, 6
Style, 56
Sunrises and sunsets, 79
Super Quad Pixel, 3
Super Slow-Mo, 35, 36
SUPER SLOW-MO, 36

SUPER SLOW-MO option, 36
supports Super HDR, 1
Swipe to **MORE**, 22
swipe up or down on the Home screen, 6
Swiping your finger up or down, 24
switch off dual recording, 25
Symmetry, 112
synchronize projects across all platforms, 60

T

Take paranoma, 29
take wide-angle, 27
taking a video, 15, 69
taking selfies, 15
Tap Camera, 29
Tap **Capture**, 6
Tap **Create album**., 44
Tap **Download**., 72
Tap icons and browse, 72
tap **MANUAL**, 33
tap on **night mode**, 13
Tap on the **Effect** icon, 22
tap Record., 8
Tap the back icon, 42
Tap the **Camera icon**., 29
tap the camera symbol, 5
Tap the **Canvas** option, 92
Tap the **Create** button, 45
Tap the **MORE** buttons, 35, 36
Tap the record button, 41
Tap the record icon, 76
Tap the settings cog, 42
Tap the **Share icon**, 29
Tap the **Single Take**, 15
Tap the **Single Take option**, 15
Tap the specific segment, 92
tap the **Stop icon**, 29
Tap the stop icon, 41
Tap the timer icon, 42
tap **Themes**, 72
tap **Video**, 29

tapping the **App to Layer** icon, 67
Telephone Mode, 79
Telephoto lenses, 3, 79
the **"Camera"** app, 6
the "Install" Option, 90
The 10-megapixel telephoto, 3
The 10-megapixel telephoto camera, 3
The 12-megapixel, 2
The 12-megapixel ultra-wide, 2
The 12-megapixel ultra-wide camera, 2
the 4K video resolution, 60
The act of composing, 118
The act of composing and shooting, 118
The act of composing and shooting the picture, 118
the **Add albums** button, 46
the app called Gallery, 26
The app features a function, 65
the **Apply** button, 72, 74, 78
the app's features., 3
the aspect ratio dimension, 59
the aspect ratio dimension of your choice., 59
the Auto Frame feature, 16
the Auto Frame function, 17
the available options, 29, 31, 50
the back camera and the selfie camera, 24
the best phones, 119
the best photo, 27
the bokeh effect, 78
the built-up hype, 1
the camera app, 19, 51, 76, 86, 98, 114
the Camera app, 7, 11, 18, 22, 24, 27, 35, 36, 51, 69, 77
The Camera Assistance App, 89
the cameras on the S23, 1, 3
the cameras on the S23 and S23 Plus, 1
the **Capture** button, 6, 31, 70
the centre of the display, 28
the circular frame, 31
the composition of the shot, 20
the **customize symbol**, 15, 28
the Director's View, 24
the editing applications, 118

The emoji, 50, 52
the **Emoji tool**, 59
The emoji's face overlays, 50
the **eraser icon**, 56
The Expert RAW, 9
The Expert RAW software, 9
the exposure value, 33, 34
The extra wide lens, 2
The final product, 13
The final product is colourful, 13
the flip symbol, 15
The front-facing camera, 15
the Galaxy S22 lineup., 1
the Galaxy S22 Ultra's, 3
The Galaxy S23 series, 1, 13
the Galaxy S23 series's rear cameras, 1
the Gallery, 8, 43, 44, 45, 46, 47, 50, 51, 54, 55, 56, 57, 66, 70, 71, 78, 95
the Gallery and appreciate, 43
the Gallery app, 8, 45, 47, 54, 55, 56, 57, 70, 71
The goal of a time-lapse movie, 38
the GoPro family of action, 40
the GoPro family of action cameras., 40
the HDR option, 86
the home screen, 29, 31, 41, 46, 68, 90
the Home screen, 28, 46, 72, 74
the icon, 8, 25, 27, 44, 50, 54, 55, 56, 57, 59, 72, 73, 92, 95, 99
The kind of outcomes, 28
the length of the video, 58
the lens is spotless, 117
the level of depth, 32
the **Lock Screen**, 5
the lower-left to view the video., 29
The main attraction, 3
The main camera, 12
the main video of the rear-view, 25
the mode menu, 31
the most recent modification, 44
the native camera app, 3
The new camera, 1
the new selfie camera's capacity, 1
the Night Portrait, 11, 18

The Night shot, 11
the Night shot icon, 7, 11
The Night shot icon, 11
the original colour, 55
the **Play** button on the video, 70
the Power button, 5
the preview thumbnail, 30, 41
the **record** button, 50, 51
the Resolution icon, 69
the S22 and S23 series, 25
The S22 boasts a selfie, 1
The S22 boasts a selfie camera, 1
the S23 series, 6, 11, 18
The S23 Series, 49
The S23 series' Object, 11
The S23 series' Object Image, 11
the S23 Ultra, 1, 3, 11, 18
the Samsung Galaxy S23 Series, 119
The Samsung S23 Ultra, 1
the **Scene optimizer**, 79
the Scene Optimizer, 13
The scene optimizer, 78
the **Scissors icon**, 58
The second telephoto camera, 4
the selfie front view, 25
The shutter on the camera, 14
the single telephoto, 4
the single telephoto camera, 4
the **Split icon**, 25
the **Stop** button, 7, 18, 53
the **stop icon**, 76
the telephoto lens, 24, 79
the Transition screen, 96
The triple rear cameras, 1
the Ultra's new front camera, 1
The use of beauty filters, 118
The video clips, 91
the **Video** option., 90
three back cameras, 3
Through the Lock Screen, 5
TikTok, 1, 63, 64, 65
Timelapse, 38, 39, 40
Timelapse Photography, 38
timelapses compress time, 38

toolbar, 25, 40, 92, 93, 94, 95
top-right corner, 28
Transform tool, 58, 59
Tress, 79
trim, 70, 96, 113
Trim the length, 58
Trim the length of a video, 58
trimming, 63, 66
turning off Dual recording, 26
Turning on the Auto Frame option, 16
two S23 series phones, 3
two telephoto cameras, 4
typical selfie, 102

U

Ultra 5G to capture, 32
Ultra's four rear cameras, 3
Ultra's four rear cameras include a 200-megapixel, 3
Ultra's four rear cameras include a 200-megapixel main camera, 3
Ultra's main camera, 3
Ultra's main camera employs, 3
Ultra's main camera employs pixel, 3
Ultra's new front, 1
unexpected movements, 11, 18
usage of the selfie camera, 24
Use a Gallery widget, 46
Use a Tripod, 102
USE ASTROPHOTOGRAPHY MODE, 14
USE AUTO FRAME, 16
USE AUTO FRAME FOR VIDEOS, 16
Use Flash only during the day, 114
USE FOOD MODE, 31
USE FOOD MODE TO CAPTURE, 31
USE FOOD MODE TO CAPTURE FLAVOR, 31
Use grid lines to balance your shots, 98
Use Guidelines, 110
Use HDR mode., 99
Use natural light., 100
Use negative spaces, 103
Use Portrait video, 22
Use Single Take, 27
USE SINGLE TAKE, 15
use the camera, 5, 14

USES OF AR ZONE, 49
USES OF AR ZONE IN S23, 49
Using AR emoji stickers, 52
Using AR emoji stickers in chats, 52
using Night movie mode, 7
USING SAMSUNG EXPERT, 80
USING SAMSUNG EXPERT RAW, 80
USING SAMSUNG EXPERT RAW TO IMPROVE YOUR PHOTOGRAPHY, 80
using the 200MP lens, 32
Using the Apps menu, 6
USING THE CAMERA, 18
USING THE CAMERA APP, 18
USING THE CAMERA APP ON GALAXY S23, 18
USING THE CAMERA APP ON GALAXY S23 SERIES, 18
USING THE CAMERA APP ON GALAXY S23 SERIES MODELS, 18
Using the Food Mode, 31
USING THE GALLERY APP, 43
USING THE GALLERY APP ON A SMARTPHONE, 43
USING THE GALLERY APP ON A SMARTPHONE OR TABLET, 43
utilize Single Shot, 3
utilize Single Shot mode, 3

V

variety of editing tools, 65
VARIOUS CAMERA, 76
various camera lenses, 24
VARIOUS CAMERA MODES, 76
VARIOUS CAMERA MODES & HOW TO USE THEM, 76
various choices, 9
Vehicle, 79
video aspect ratio, 63, 64
video collages, 64
Video Editing, 57
VIDEO icon., 7

video images, 27
video recording, 11, 18
Video Recording, 87
Video Recording in Photo Mode, 87
Video recording in Photo mode., 86
Video shooting mode, 16
video stabilizer, 61
view live thumbnails, 53
viewfinder of the camera, 25
Viewing and editing photos and videos, 43
VivaCut, 64
Vlogger, 53
Vlogger mode, 53
Vloggers, 53
voiceovers to videos, 64

W

watch button, 76
Watersides, 79
What are the 4 ways to launch the Galaxy, 5
What is Super Slow-Mo?, 35
What is Time-lapse?, 38
Where can I find the different camera modes and can I download more?, 76
While shooting a movie, 52
White Balance, 33, 84
works with HD resolution, 35

Y

year's lineup, 1
YouTube, 1, 29, 63, 64, 66, 69, 71, 92, 94

Z

zoom in, 4, 6, 7, 16, 17, 20, 21, 29, 79, 92, 113
Zoom-in mic, 29

Made in the USA
Columbia, SC
09 December 2024

48880294R00076